To Dad   Dec, 2001

I love you

Lo

Kundalini Energy

The Flame of Life

Mary Ellen Flora

You, the spirit, may develop and flourish in conjunction with the proper care of your body and mind. Therefore, the information in this publication is intended to assist you in your spiritual development and to enhance, but not be substituted for, any care you should receive from your licensed healthcare or mental health professional for the treatment of pain or any other symptom or condition.

First Printing 1998

Printed on recycled paper in the United States of America
Malloy Lithographing Inc., Ann Arbor, Michigan

Library of Congress Catalog Card Number: 98-72488

ISBN 1-886983-07-0

THIS BOOK IS DEDICATED
TO LIFE!

Hebrew: L'chiam!

Chinese: Shēnghuó kuàilè!

Estonian: Elagu!

Filipino: Mabuhay!

French: Vive la vie!

German: Auf das Leben!

Hindi: jīte raho!

Italian: Viva la vita!

Japanese: subarasii jinsei-ni kanpai

Russian: Za zheezn!

Spanish: ¡Viva la vida!

Swahili: Kwa maisha!

IN EVERY LANGUAGE,
TO LIFE!

Thank you to Barbara Blair for an excellent job leading the production of this book. Many thanks to Carrie Harris for her beautiful graphic design for the cover and throughout the book, as well as for the technical work.

Thank you to Lembi Kongas for an excellent job editing, doing research, and for advice and joyous participation.

Thank you to "Doc" for his loving encouragement and assistance.

Thank you to Diane Brewster and Diane Olson for proofreading, and to Stacy Rice, Kim Zirbes and Jeff Rice for technical assistance.

Thanks to Johanna Stark for her contribution of artwork. Also thanks to Judy Henceroth for support in general services.

Many thanks to the C.D.M. community for financial and energetic assistance and encouragement. I appreciate the help and encouragement given by the Board of Directors and many others in C.D.M. I especially want to thank Diane and Cory Olson, Marie and Dave Senestraro, Pamela Lynn, and Stacy and Jeff Rice for their generous financial support.

I thank God for the call and the information to write this book and the support of a powerful spiritual community to make it physically possible.

TABLE OF CONTENTS

INTRODUCTION

This book is dedicated to life because kundalini energy is life. Kundalini is a life-force of spirit. It is a gift from God to use while in a body. I am able to accomplish all that I do as a teacher, healer, bishop, writer, wife, administrator, friend, and all the other roles I play on Earth because I run kundalini energy. I use this spiritualizing force in everything I do and you can also. Whether you are meditating, healing, cooking a meal for your family, administering a business, or taking out the garbage, you can use kundalini energy to transform your experience to one of spiritual awareness.

However, mystery and misinformation surround kundalini energy. Many books and articles have been written about people's kundalini experiences, but few of these treatises have been simple or clear about this energy of transformation. Many people who have experienced kundalini energy and written about it have expressed their emotionality and physical experience more than their knowledge and spiritual perspective of kundalini. Others who have information about kundalini energy consider it a mystery which the individual soul must discover on its own. Thus, they either do not write about it, or they write in a mysterious manner about kundalini. Adepts have often written in Eastern terms which may be confusing to the novice. This presentation about kundalini energy provides simple, clear information that anyone can understand. It is time for information about kundalini to be available to anyone wishing to have it as it is time for the human race to gain greater spiritual maturity.

I have used kundalini energy for as long as I can remember. I have been physically conscious of the meaning and purpose of kundalini energy for over twenty years. My experience with kundalini energy has run the gamut, from disturbance to internal peace and cosmic ecstasy, and has stimulated every emotion from fear to joy. It has been a healing force throughout my life. Whether I used kundalini energy consciously or unconsciously, it has been a powerful force of spiritual energy that has helped me move through this world without having to be overwhelmed by its physical pull. Like everyone in a body, I have to balance the spirit and body dichotomy, and kundalini energy has always helped me move above the physical to regain my spiritual awareness. I am writing this book about kundalini energy because there is so much confusion and misinformation about it, and many people need to know about this revitalizing energy. Kundalini energy is affecting the lives of so many at this time of growth on Earth.

Recently, when I was doubting the call to write this book about such a powerful energy, I read an article that described a woman's kundalini experience, and it confirmed my belief that people need information about kundalini. This woman was put in the psychiatric ward of a hospital and was heavily drugged because of her bizarre behavior. She later learned that her experience stemmed from activating her kundalini energy. She proceeded to relate her entire experience to the kundalini energy instead of realizing that most of her unpleasant experience was due to what she was cleansing from her physical and spiritual system and to the way she was treated. She did not understand that the kundalini energy simply activated what she had stored in her body. Since she had a great deal of pain and disturbance in her system, she had traumatic experiences and her scientific healers were oblivious to kundalini energy and its effects. Unfortunately, she proceeded to tell frightening ideas about kundalini energy to everyone who would listen. During my years of using kundalini energy, I have never had any of the unpleasant experiences she described. Trauma does not have to be a part of your kundalini experience if you prepare your body for spiritual transformation. Kundalini energy is a catalyst; it is not what it stimulates. It is a very high energy that transforms lower energies.

I am writing this book because more and more people are spontaneously turning on their kundalini energy and do not know what is happening to them. It can be frightening when you have a powerful experience and do not understand it. This information is to help people understand the nature of kundalini, how it affects the physical body, and its spiritual purpose. Kundalini energy is a wonderful transforming energy. There is no need to be afraid of it. It is necessary to be aware of what it is and how it works. Since kundalini energy is so powerful, it is important to cleanse the physical and spiritual system as much as possible before using kundalini for your spiritual transformation. Those who prepare do not have traumatic experiences. People who do not operate as spirit and neglect to prepare their system experience disturbances and sometimes trauma, as did the woman who had the frightening experience.

We are meant to live fully in these physical bodies, and kundalini energy is not intended to turn us into celibate saints, unless that is our desire. Kundalini energy is meant to help us awaken to the fact that we are spirit creating in the physical world and to help us transform our physical creations to a higher vibration which is easier for us to flow through as spirit. We can use our kundalini energy to meditate and communicate with the Cosmic Consciousness or to heal our bodies or to play a sport. This wonderful energy is for our spiritual creativity in the physical world. It is a cosmic energy we can use in our physical body to create in any manner.

I live what most people would consider a normal life,

with home and family, work, hobbies, sports, and quiet time. I enjoy food, wine, laughter, and fun. Kundalini energy is one of the forces that allows me to enjoy life to its fullest. It energizes and cleanses my body, enhances my spiritual awareness, and gives me the energy to participate fully in life. Whether I am trying to win at tennis with my young niece or in a deep meditation with my God, kundalini energy is a major part of the fuel of my spiritual fire.

The world is full of beauty and you can learn to see it when you tune into God and your spiritual nature. I wish to encourage everyone who will listen to turn within to the power of God that is within you. By quieting your physical creations and paying attention to your spiritual nature, you can cleanse and prepare yourself for spiritual awakening. Your kundalini energy is a major part of your transformation. Kundalini helps you experience the spiritual nature of all things, from the mundane to the sublime.

Let go of your expectations and fears, and join me on a journey into spiritual awareness where life is full of energy, discovery, and joy.

KUNDALINI, THE TRANSFORMER

Kundalini is a spiritual energy which is meant to transform our physical creations to a higher vibration. Everything is energy. Albert Einstein's discovery that $E = mc^2$ means that energy equals matter moving at the speed of light. Simply stated, matter is slow moving energy. Physical matter is so slow moving that we can see it with our physical eyes. Physical matter is a lower and slower vibration than pure spiritual energy. Spirit is a fast moving energy that is not usually seen by the physical eyes. Kundalini energy helps bring these two vibrations, high and low, together. The kundalini flow of energy through the body helps bring the physical vibration up so the high vibration of spirit can more easily flow through the physical form. Kundalini energy unites the spiritual with the physical.

Kundalini means "coiled up." It is like a coiled snake in its characteristics and is often depicted in the image of a coiled snake in Eastern religions. Kundalini energy is dormant until stimulated by a soul's conscious preparation or unconscious actions and behavior. It can be quiet for a long time, and then "uncoil" suddenly and frighten the body with its speed and power. Kundalini energy is latent in every person. Everything is energy, and kundalini is the energy transformer available to everyone. It takes several lifetimes for a soul to consciously control its kundalini energy, but it may arise at any time depending on the soul's development, focus, or desire.

You must constantly evaluate your beliefs, ideas, and concepts when focusing on a spiritual path. Spiritual growth provides a great challenge to stay in control and on your true path. Kundalini energy moves you along so rapidly, you must stay spiritually focused to remain true to yourself. The physical world offers many temptations, and kundalini energy speeds up their presentation, so you need information rapidly. Ask yourself what your reasons are for wanting to turn on your kundalini. If you do not know yourself, you may need to meditate for some time before focusing on your kundalini energy.

Kundalini energy transforms what you, the spirit, have created in physical matter into spiritual energy. If you have created a healthy body full of affinity, happiness, and joy, your kundalini energy will immediately translate this energy to a higher vibration for you, as spirit, to flow into and through. If you have created pain, misery, and fear, your kundalini energy will translate these into a higher vibration; this means you will have to begin your transformation with intense healing work. There is a drastic difference between the two extremes just described. Most people are somewhere in between with both joy and sadness, fear and love, and pain and happiness. The nature of the transformation caused by kundalini energy is dependent on your creativity. If you have created clarity, the transformation will be easy. If you have created a system cluttered with debilitating energies, you will have a challenging or difficult transformation.

You, the spirit, are the creator of your reality in the physical world. You are energy and you use energy to create in matter. Once you have manifested into matter at your conception and come into the material reality at your birth, you continue to create your beliefs into material form through your physical body.[1] The kundalini process helps you transform your energy into the physical form, and then transforms whatever you have created in the physical form back into spiritual energy. The most obvious times you accomplish this transformation are when you come into the body at birth and when you leave your body at death.

Some souls use kundalini energy at conception and birth to help them bring more of their energy into the body at the beginning of their earthly experience. A man I knew many years ago had great difficulty getting space from his mother as she had a kundalini experience during his birth and believed that he was the Christ child. She saw colors around him when he was born and saw colors in her own head during the birth. She had an experience of spiritual ecstasy and believed it indicated the divinity of her child. She did not know that everyone is divine, so she thought her child was special. As an adult, her son sought spiritual information to explain her experiences at his birth in order to save himself from his mother's expectations. Even though he learned about kundalini energy and how it affected his birth and taught her about its effects, she did not want to give up her ideals about her son. She enjoyed following him around so much that she did not want to change her game. Kundalini energy is often misunderstood and can also be misused.

Other souls do not become acquainted with kundalini energy until later in their physical life. Many souls do not begin this transformation of spiritualizing the physical body until they are older. They are busy creating into matter during the earlier part of their incarnation and do not realize they can consciously use spiritual energy throughout life. The soul creates the body and develops it into physical maturity. In adult life, the soul creates work, family, and other extensions of itself. The vibrations it uses and the things it creates depend on the soul's beliefs. The soul's creativity is an expression of the beliefs it brings into the body, what it learns in the body, and what it adopts from others. The soul's beliefs and the energy it uses to manifest those beliefs physically is what has to be transformed back into pure spiritual energy. What the soul invests in matter must be retrieved.

Kundalini energy is the transformer that changes all

that a soul has invested into the physical realm back into
cosmic energy. Kundalini energy transforms the physical
back into the spiritual form of pure energy. Kundalini
energy raises the vibrations used to create matter in the
physical plane to a spiritual state where the energy can be
used by the soul in other ways and in other lives.
Kundalini is the transforming energy that helps us, as
spirit, to move into and out of the physical world, as well
as to create in a spiritually aware state while in a body.

Kundalini energy is neutral. It does not have body
characteristics such as emotions, sexuality, and pain. It is
a neutral energy, much like electricity. Kundalini energy
moves through the spiritual system and body and
stimulates the body's existing characteristics. Like
electricity, kundalini energy is not conscious; it is simply
a powerful energy. It is up to the individual soul to learn
to be conscious of and in control of its kundalini energy.

Kundalini energy manifests itself in infinite ways. You
can learn to identify how it affects you and your body.
The first time you consciously turn on your kundalini,
you may have the experience of saying to yourself, "Oh,
that's what that is." Kundalini energy can cause physical,
emotional, and psychological responses from your body,
so it is important to learn how to control it in order for
the kundalini energy not to control you. Kundalini has a
powerful impact on the body since it is changing every
cell in the body.

You need to develop your use of kundalini energy

slowly and carefully as it affects all of your chakras or spiritual energy centers, the rest of your spiritual system, and your entire body system. Kundalini energy has a major impact on you, as spirit, and on all of your creativity, including your body. It is best to learn about your chakras and how to meditate on them before consciously turning on your kundalini energy.[2] All of the chakras are stimulated by the kundalini energy, so you need to understand the chakra system to fully comprehend what is happening with your kundalini transformation.

Kundalini energy is often experienced during birth and death since these are the transition points into and out of the physical body. The soul needs a high vibration to make this transition from the spiritual to the physical realm, and then out of the physical back to the spiritual. Societies that are aware of the spiritual nature of humanity have rituals surrounding birth and death which assist the soul in these times of transition. Unfortunately, in technological society our attention is focused on the intellectual arena and our awareness is dimmed to the spiritual nature of birth, life, and death. We are now focused on the body rather than the spirit which causes us to be survival-oriented rather than focused on spiritual creativity.

We are spirit and are here on Earth to learn about creativity. When we put our attention on only one of our creations, the body, we focus on its main interest, which is survival. This obsession with survival keeps us from experiencing the joy and enthusiasm which is possible when we are focused on spirit and God. All of the world religions were intended to remind us of our spiritual nature. Unfortunately, each one has developed many worldly patterns focusing on the intellect and survival instincts. The original teachings all focused on our spiritual nature while the present organizations representing the teachings also focus on survival issues such as exclusivity, physical characteristics, ethics, the intellect, territory, dogma, ritual, and other body-oriented issues.

God continues to send us teachers, signs, spiritual information, revelations, and other messages to help us wake up to the fact that we are spirit and not the bodies we create and inhabit. Kundalini energy is one of the vibrations to help us experience and maintain our spiritual awareness and vitality while in a body. The existence, purpose, and use of kundalini energy is not taught by most of the world religions. In fact, the truth about kundalini energy is kept as secret as possible by many of the religious powers. Some of the groups which are aware of and publicly use kundalini energy do not teach the masses of humanity that we can all use this energy to manifest a more spiritually focused life. Many of the priesthoods of this world are not sharing all they know as they have become engulfed by the physical world and its obsession with survival. Since knowledge is power, many groups now play power games with their information instead of the originally intended game of encouraging spiritual enlightenment.

Kundalini energy can raise the individual soul above the survival level of life on Earth into a state of spiritual awareness. If this is the case for every soul, what purpose would we have for many religious organizations as they exist today? If a religious organization does not offer community, support for the individual's relationship with God, and instruction for spiritual creativity and communication, what is its purpose? Kundalini raises the awareness above the need for guilt, fear, control games, and other manipulations that have become popular with religious powers over the centuries. Religions are ideally meant to inspire, encourage, and instruct; not to chastise, condemn, or punish. Kundalini energy frees us from earthly games.

Kundalini energy is the neutral transformer. It transforms the individual into an awakened state, and it will in time transform the planet and all of its institutions into an awakened reality. Every individual soul who consciously uses kundalini energy helps to raise the vibration of Earth. As the Earth raises its vibration, the consciousness of every soul is affected. Kundalini helps one see truth, thus it is a challenge to use this energy if lies are the norm.

You may have a great deal of your spiritual energy invested in survival-oriented creations such as being good, earning money, buying things, being concerned about what others think of you, and other body focuses. You can raise these survival issues to a different plane of reality by learning to use your kundalini energy consciously. Creating in a physical body does not have to be survival-oriented if you maintain a spiritual perspective. Kundalini energy helps you gain and keep your spiritual awareness and vitality. Even in a survival situation such as war, famine, or other circumstance of deprivation, you can use your kundalini energy to move through the experience with a spiritual perspective and grace.

It is extremely important to evaluate your reasons for awakening and using kundalini energy. "Know yourself" is taught by every great teacher. Knowing yourself is vital when awakening your kundalini energy. Kundalini has the power to awaken what you have created, so you need to know who you are, what you have created, and your purpose on Earth. Kundalini energy will introduce you to yourself and your creations rapidly. You may need time to prepare your body before focusing on kundalini energy, so your body will not be frightened when you do. Meditation is the best way to prepare.

If you know that you have emotional or physical pain in your body from past injuries, you will understand when the pain is stimulated, and you can release it without resistance. If you are unaware of a disturbance in your system, you may fight it, believing it has an external source. Your fight and resistance will create more pain and disturbance if you are using kundalini. You must be able to let go rapidly to effectively use this powerful energy because kundalini has no ethics. It moves through the system without concern for pain, emotions, sexuality, ethics, or anything else it stimulates to transform. Kundalini, the transformer, is a spiritual force that we need to learn to consciously and safely use.

Kundalini energy can be a part of life for anyone on Earth. It is not something for special people; it is for all people who wish to do the work to awaken and control it. Kundalini energy is a gift from God to help us create the world of matter, and then to rise above the physical world we have created to remember that we are spirit and the creators of our reality. It is a gift of energy to help us regain the spiritual energy we have invested in the material world. Kundalini energy helps us reunite our consciousness with the Cosmic Consciousness.

SPIRIT IS SIMPLE

Spirit is simple and the body is complex. You are spirit and you have a body. You, as spirit, are seen as a bright spark of light in this physical reality. Your body is your spiritual creation and your physical "home" through which you create and communicate. You are pure energy and your body is the energy you have invested into the material world; therefore, you, as spirit, move much faster than your slow moving material body. Your body is a composite of your information which you store and manifest in many forms. You create your life from and through the beliefs you have in your body and your spiritual system.

Spirit creates in the physical world, and form manifests. Spirit "desires" something, and it happens. Spirit creates with desire and belief. Spirit also destroys with its desires and beliefs. The process of creating and destroying is continuous for spirit. When spirit is outside of a body, this cycle of creating and destroying is not limited by physical rules such as ethics, time, and effort. Spirit continues to do this when it is in a body and, in this manner, creates its reality. When the spirit enters a body, the creative game is complicated by the existing physical environment. Spirit without a body creates and destroys, at will, without limits. Spirit with a body is creating through a complex material system and has to re-learn how to use the system without giving up its spiritual creative freedom. Most souls forget who they are and get lost in the physical system. For example, a spirit wants to learn about power in the material world, so it creates a physical body to learn the appropriate lessons. The spirit brings its beliefs from previous lives, adopts beliefs from parents and other life teachers, and creates new beliefs in the present body. These beliefs create the medium through which the spirit creates. If the spirit believes that power is strictly a physical issue, it will not use its spiritual abilities to learn about power. If the spirit believes its spiritual nature can manifest in the physical realm, it will use its spiritual abilities to learn about power in the physical world. Whatever its beliefs, whether created or adopted, they influence its experience. If the spirit believes it must work hard to have power, it will create that experience. Thus, the desires and the beliefs of the spirit create its experience in the physical world. It is important to remember that beliefs and even desires can be changed.

The more complex the belief system, the more complex the experience. If a spirit believes it must take twenty steps to arrive at its goal, then it will take twenty steps. If it believes it only has to take one step to accomplish the task, then one step will do. The spirit usually builds and adopts a complex set of beliefs to establish itself in the material world and forgets its spiritual simplicity. Most of the physical world is steeped in complex sets of beliefs. Study any nation, religion, neighborhood, family, or other social system, and you will discover a complex system of beliefs. Spirit is simply a part of God. Spirit creates the body and becomes involved in family, community, education, religion, and other belief systems to learn and create as much as possible. Spirit is immortal and the body is mortal; thus, spirit is eternal, while the body strives to survive.

A significant purpose of the spirit coming into a body is to learn to spiritualize the body system for spirit to use to create and communicate. Kundalini energy helps you bring the vibration of the body up to a level where you, as spirit, can use it more effectively. Kundalini energy clears out the complexities you have stored in your body and allows your energy to move freely through the body. This energy lets you, the spirit, regain control over your material creations instead of continuing to allow your body and your creations to control you. You, as spirit, know that you are a part of God. You may have adopted the belief that you must say prayers, confess sins, and use an intermediary in some priesthood to relate to God. You, as spirit, have a simple one-to-one relationship with God but may have created or adopted a complex system in the body to make it feel real in the physical world. You can cleanse this complex system and allow the simple knowledge that you are part of God by using your spiritual energies to clear the physical beliefs. Kundalini energy is one of the most effective energies to use for the cleansing and healing process. With your spiritual perspective, you can see how to use your religion to relate to God instead of to the physical complexities.

The differences between spirit and body are a significant factor in the confusion about spiritual growth and development. The body is the vehicle for the spirit in the material world, and thus operates in the physical system. Bodies operate through time and space. Bodies have weight and mass. Bodies communicate with emotions and the intellect. The main concern of the body is survival, thus it creates ethical systems and competition to establish its survival needs such as territory. Every action by a physical body requires effort. The body requires time to create.

The body is a marvelous machine which is a physical creation for spirit to use. It has characteristics that are unique to the body and ways of operating which are strictly physical. The body experiences pain. It has an entire spectrum of emotions from apathy to enthusiasm. The body is mortal; it dies. The body is of the physical world and needs to relate to the physical reality.

Spirit has none of the above characteristics. Spirit is immortal, neutral, and all-knowing. Spirit is not limited by time, space, or mass. Spirit creates instantly. Spirit does not have emotions, pain, or effort. Spirit and body are opposite. Spirit has to either remember or re-learn how to use a physical body each time it takes one. This knowledge that spirit and body are different is essential in one's spiritual development. Since kundalini energy brings spirit and body together, it is essential to know and respect the characteristics of both.

Many bright spirits have awakened, and then lost themselves in the body's way of operating. One young man I know created beautiful music which was obviously spiritually inspired. He used spiritual techniques, including his kundalini energy, while creating the music. He was like Icarus who flew too close to the sun and fell to Earth. He flew high spiritually and physically, but forgot that he was also influenced by his body's survival drive. He eventually lost the flow of inspiration he was receiving because he followed his temptations instead of his spiritual path. In his "fall to Earth," he hurt himself and other people.

It is essential to stay clear about your purpose and beliefs when using kundalini energy. You are moving so fast that if you step off your path, you can be in another world very quickly. The young man was in a world of music, joy, and creativity one moment and was in another world in only a few months. He did not clear his system of hate, fear, and pain, and these physical pulls rapidly dominated his creativity. He was easily led from his path by his physical characteristics of competition, ego, and sexuality. Instead of cleansing his body and raising his energy, he used the power of his kundalini energy to create his body's desires.

Spirit is here on Earth to create, learn, and grow. Spirit can learn about its body and how to use it and even to be senior to it. Spirit can learn to control the body. Many beings learn to control the body to use it fully for their spiritual purpose. When embarking on a spiritual path, such as using kundalini energy, spirit must always be aware of the body and the body's influence on its creativity. Without this awareness of physical pulls, spirit can easily get lost in worldly pursuits instead of focusing on spiritual goals.

Spiritual seekers can have a joyous experience. I have enjoyed watching students enter spiritual training and move from a complex, disturbing way of life to a simpler spiritual way of living. It is not always obvious when this occurs, but sometimes it is a transition that cannot be missed. A friend of mine is a good example of an obvious change in her life from complex to simple, from body to spiritual focus. She was involved with many men, focused her attention on her physical beauty and physical accomplishments. She sought money, sex, and excitement. She believed that her information was outside of her, and thus looked to others for her information and validation. She had a busy life trying to figure out what other people wanted her to do and how they wanted her to act. After several years of spiritual focus, she began to turn within to her own information, and her interests changed. She began to pay more attention to healing herself and others and less attention to pleasing everyone. Her old friends disappeared as she no longer partied all night or went out to bars to find entertainment and validation. She grew spiritually to the point that she was able to ask God for guidance in selecting a mate. Soon after she did this, she realized that she was in love with a man she had known for years as a friend. Her life is no longer scattered and disrupted by a search outside herself.

This woman is now focused on herself and her spiritual creativity. She has created a family, become a spiritual teacher, and is focused on the development of a spiritual community. She moved from a focus on the body and outside sources of information, which made her life complex and scattered, to an internal spiritual focus. Her life is more centered and gaining simplicity. In her process of spiritual growth, she has influenced many other people to slow down and pay attention to what is important. This friend is a great joy in my life and has helped me slow down and pay attention several times.

Many people have come into classes burdened with complex beliefs and lives. They have been trying to solve other people's problems, trying to please everyone but themselves, trying to change the world. They were not aware of themselves as spirit. The most important information they receive is that they are spirit and not their body or their creations. Many of these people begin to simplify life immediately just by realizing they do not have to do all of the physical things they believed they were required to do. Many students discover that life can become simple instead of complex by changing their beliefs and increasing their spiritual awareness.

When you operate as spirit, you stay in tune with your spiritual self and information. You follow your spiritual path and do not get absorbed by the physical systems around you. Look at your world and all of the complexities in it, and you will see there is more than you can physically accomplish. If you regain your spiritual perspective, you will see that you, as spirit, can accomplish what you are here to do if you give up the complexities you have superimposed on your path. You may discover, from a spiritual perspective, that the physical complexities are not important to you.

A young woman I know was spiritually merged with her mother because she was trying to solve her mother's problems. This woman tried to solve her spiritual problem in a physical manner and made her own life very complex. She tried to physically separate herself from her mother, so she traveled to several different countries in the attempt to be herself instead of her mother's clone. She eventually discovered that she is spirit and realized that she needed to make a spiritual, rather than a physical, separation between herself and her mother. When she did this, she was able to stop running. She has settled in a community, bought a house, and gotten married since she stopped physically running away from her mother and the belief that she had to heal her mother. This young woman grew up when she acknowledged the spiritual nature of both herself and her mother. Her life is much simpler since she has a place to live, stability for her physical creativity, and freedom from trying to solve someone else's problems.

The more complex the beliefs, the more complex the life. My young friend had an unbelievable number of expectations about herself and others, which confused her about who she was and what she wanted to do. She simplified her life by releasing the expectations she had learned from others and the ones she had created for herself. When she stopped checking with everyone about whether or not she was all right, she was able to see what she wanted and what the right thing was for her. Her creativity became focused in one place and in one direction instead of in many places and directions. She began to do what she wanted to do, instead of what everyone else wanted her to do.

Developing a spiritual perspective is an important part of gaining seniority with the body and making life simple. Meditation is the easiest route to a spiritual perspective. Meditation helps you learn about yourself so you can create the simplicity of spirit in your life. Meditate on one thing in your life to see how you can make it simple. If you have so many responsibilities at work and home that you do not have time for yourself, meditate on what is important to you. As you gain your spiritual perspective, you may begin to let go of things you once believed were of great importance. You may even realize that the world can get along without you long enough for you to have some quiet time to talk with yourself and God.

Many people have to change a few beliefs to begin meditating. A friend recently broke his leg in an accident while playing golf. He is a teacher, so the injury interfered with his work schedule. He was accustomed to a very active life of tennis, golf, and other sports as well as his busy teaching schedule. When I was visiting him, I gave his leg a spiritual healing to help the movement of energy and assist the healing process. I mentioned to him that he was learning about what was important to him. He agreed and commented that during his recuperation, he realized how unimportant many things were that he had believed were significant to him. He saw how unnecessary many aspects of his life really were when going to the bathroom, walking, and other things he took for granted became his main concern.

This man is a wonderful healer who is always working with people and giving to others. His injury was clearly an opportunity for him to turn within and learn something about himself, as a healer. He came to realize that he had to heal himself first. As he focused on healing his injured leg, he learned to know himself better, especially his healing qualities. He is learning how to receive as he balances his energy and heals himself. He has simplified his life by allowing others to give to him and help him. He no longer believes he has to do everything for everyone.

Kundalini energy can help with this process of bringing the simplicity of spirit back into your life. Most spirits create and create in the physical world, without consideration of their spiritual nature, until they are buried in their physical creations. Kundalini energy helps with the clean-up process and with the revitalization of the physical system. It brings the spiritual vitality back into the spirit's creative process. As kundalini energy flows through the body, it transforms the energy invested in physical form back to spiritual vitality, which then can be used by the spirit for its purpose. Kundalini helps unify and bridge the differences between spirit and body as it brings the energy of the body up for spirit to easily use.

Simplicity is a joy and complexity can be a burden. We can create in the physical world with the simplicity of spirit. We do not have to make everything complex. We can bring spirit and God into our lives by learning to use kundalini energy and other spiritual techniques to transform our awareness from physical to spiritual. With the spiritual perspective, all of our physical creations take on a transformed meaning. For example, we see our children not as a burden, but as a gift from God; our mate not as someone we have to tolerate, but as someone to love and be loved by; ourselves not as insignificant and alone, but as a part of God. The simple view of spirit always includes spirit and God. The complex view of the body includes everything within and around the body. The spiritual view has a simple answer, and the physical view provides complex, emotional, and intellectual options.

One question can help you see the difference. For example, how can I find the right life partner? The body's complex system may suggest singles' bars, computer dating, church socials, blind dates, or any number of other ideas to try to find this elusive person. Spirit would meditate and know an answer to the question. The answer could be patience, heal yourself, or become aware of a friend in a different light. The physical view looks outside of self and the spiritual one looks within. All of your answers are within you. All of your information can be viewed simply as spirit.

The complexities we have created in the body such as ethics, social systems, religions, and governments are part of our spiritual creativity. To best use the physical system, we need to operate as spirit and move above it to a spiritual perspective. The body needs rules to live by if spirit is absent, since the body's survival drive is so strong it would take over and operate without thought to kindness, creativity, or love. The body, without spirit, would focus only on survival.

The next time you have a decision to make, let go of the complex decision-making process of the body and try the formula of simplicity. Stop trying to figure out what others want or think, what the rules are, or what you should do, and tune into yourself as spirit and what your purpose is here on Earth. Stop thinking, and meditate on the correct course for you, and your spiritual answers will come to you. Let go of the intellectual, emotional complexities of the body, and you will discover the simple, clear information which you have as spirit. Kundalini energy can help you with this process, but you, as spirit, must make a commitment to stay focused on your spiritual instead of your physical creativity.

> *"Kundalini energy is a stimulant to the experience of spiritual ecstasy."*

THE ECSTASY OF
SPIRITUAL EXPERIENCE

A verbal description of ecstasy is ridiculous, but the written word is all I have for use here. Therefore, I will tell you about some of my experiences, provide some general information about ecstasy, and share some other people's stories about ecstasy. Remember that ecstasy is a personal experience and will be unique to every soul. One soul may experience a state of spiritual ecstasy during meditation while another soul may experience something similar while out hiking in a beautiful place, looking at the stars at night, doing some favorite thing, or by not doing anything at all. Kundalini energy is a stimulant to the experience of spiritual ecstasy.

You are unlikely to instantly create ecstasy any more than you instantly create romance, although both of these are possible. It takes time to create in the physical world. You can create the most beneficial setting for the experience of either romance or ecstasy and allow it to emerge. If you want a romantic interlude, you may create an atmosphere with a candlelight dinner with wine and flowers. But, as everyone knows, this does not guarantee romance. The setting could generate a philosophical, angry, affectionate, or quiet interaction, or any other kind of interaction. The desire and the setting are not enough to create your romance. You also need to believe that you can create this romance. This means you are willing to create many different settings or the same setting more than once to create what you want. The desire for something and the belief you can create it allow it to happen in time.

Whether in romance or in spiritual development, you need to be patient and faithful to your desire for it to manifest in the body. You need to believe in what you desire and allow time so it can manifest in the physical world. You can set the stage to experience spiritual ecstasy by meditating, but meditation does not guarantee ecstasy. Your meditation may stimulate the anger you have stored in your body, which will then interfere with the experience of ecstasy. If you resist the anger or try to pretend that it does not exist in you, then you will move farther from ecstasy instead of closer to it. Just as you would move farther from your romantic interlude if you ignored anger between you and your partner, rather than confronting it and moving through it.

Those who seek romance often find it elusive. Those who seek spiritual ecstasy usually find it elusive also. The best way I know to experience either of these desired experiences is to learn to know yourself. You may think this is a long route to your goal, but it is the only one I know. You must know that you are spirit, a part of the Cosmic Consciousness, and not your body. You need to learn about your unique vibration and how to allow it to flow through your body. You need to learn how to ground your vibration into the physical world and how to control the energy so you can create what you want. You need to learn how to operate your body and what you have stored in it. There is so much to know about yourself. Fortunately, learning about yourself is the most fascinating thing there is to do.

There is an old saying, "You don't attract what you want, but what you are." This is true in romance and in spiritual development. You create through your spiritual creation, your body. Your unique spiritual vibration moves through your physical body and what you have created and stored in your body. If you have a great deal of fear and pain in your body, you will create your relationships through this, whether the relationship is with another person or between you, as spirit, and your body. Spiritual ecstasy is an experience of you, the spirit, using your body to relate to the Cosmic Consciousness on a high energy level.

Experiencing spiritual ecstasy without the conscious participation of the physical body is easy. Bringing ecstasy into the physical realm is the difficult part. Experiencing romance outside of your body is easy also, since you can fantasize about romance. The problem is cleansing and preparing the physical body to receive and experience the spiritual energy which generates ecstasy. This process of healing the body and spiritual system is what you do as you learn to know yourself. Meditation is the best way to turn within to learn to know you. Meditation is the internal avenue to spiritual awakening and eventual ecstasy.

You have to release your expectations about ecstasy, just as you have to let go of expectations about romance. If you expect the romance to be a particular way, you block the free flow of the experience. You may have the idea that there must be candles on the table for true romance. If there are none, you will become so fixated on the lack of candles that you miss the romantic energy exuding from your partner. You can also miss your own experience with spiritual ecstasy by expecting it to be one way when it is another.

You can have everything you want by creating it within you. If you want to experience spiritual ecstasy, you must know what that is for you and clear your system of the energies you have stored within which interfere with your experience. Pain and ecstasy do not work well together, so you have to learn how to clear your pain or move above your pain. Either choice requires that you know yourself. You may discover that knowing yourself as spirit and understanding what you have created in the physical world is ecstatic in itself.

I have had many experiences that I describe as ecstatic. These experiences are outside of the intellectual, emotional levels of the physical body, so they are difficult to describe in words. As a child, I was, at times, fascinated by my experiences, and, at other times, was disturbed since there were no adults to help me understand my experiences. I was not aware what these experiences were until I was an adult. Many spiritual experiences are misunderstood as there is so little information about spirit in most of the world.

You may have had several spiritual experiences, and even experienced what you will come to call ecstasy, but were afraid of the unknown, so you disrupted or stopped the experiences. Spiritual ecstasy is not a difficult state to create once you know yourself. Some people do not realize they are learning to know themselves, and, in the process, have an ecstatic experience and believe they are sick or "crazy." The woman I mentioned at the first of the book had an ecstatic experience and stopped it instead of enjoying the experience. Her kundalini energy stimulated what was stored in her body as it raised her vibration, and it frightened her so much she attempted to stop the process.

Kundalini energy is one of the main vibrations that helps us experience spiritual ecstasy. As kundalini energy moves through the body, it cleanses and increases the vibration of the body so it can receive your spiritual energy. The kundalini energy activates the chakras and brings out whatever you have stored within your system. If you have pain, it stimulates pain. If you have joy, it stimulates joy. It cleanses and it intensifies. Kundalini energy raises your energy through stages of awareness until eventually you see what look like heavenly stars. You may see some less pleasant things on the way to those "stars."

I have experienced the flow of kundalini energy all of my life and have had both the experience of joy and the experience of pain as it moved through my system, depending on what I was cleansing from my body at the time. I climbed trees a great deal when I was a child. Often I would climb a tree late in the day and watch the sunset as I waited for my father to come home from work. I experienced spiritual ecstasy many times during this period of my life as I focused on the horizon of blue mountains and the setting sun. I did not know the word "meditation," but that was what I did as I focused on the setting sun. I would say a prayer to God and say good night to the sun, and then become completely quiet. My experience of internal peace and fullness was a thing of quiet joy. I felt God and the spiritual communication that comes from being quiet and receiving what is given. I had the simple faith of a child and experienced the ecstasy of being part of the Whole. My kundalini energy was a part of this even though I did not know it at the time.

My body would become warm and then hot. My spine would tingle, and I would often see colors that were not obvious to the physical eye. I would hear beautiful music and singing. I felt a oneness with the world and knew my part in the whole pattern. I often wrote poems or songs after these experiences in an attempt to express my feelings. I gained joy and strength from this communication with the Cosmic Consciousness. I did not talk about my experiences as I believed they would have seemed unusual to others. I believed these experiences were my quiet time with God and hoped the world was as in tune with God as I felt.

To me this is ecstasy, to be in touch with the Cosmic Consciousness and experience oneness with all things; to melt into the Whole and know you are a part of it; to feel the joy of knowing you are a part of God. In later chapters, I will offer more technical information about kundalini energy and explain how it stimulates the chakra centers, including clairvoyance, and how it spiritualizes the physical body. Here I hope to help you realize that spiritual ecstasy can be a common occurrence and is not for a special few. Every soul can awaken its kundalini energy and use it to reunite with the Cosmic. This spiritual awareness can be discovered within everyone and can be stimulated within the body to fulfill the spiritual purpose.

One experience I had as an adult was similar to these childhood happenings. Around 11:00 p.m., on a summer night, I was meditating and was told by my spirit guides to go outside. I went into the back yard and looked at the clear night sky and saw the moon and stars shining brightly. I saw clearly that the moon is a wonderful example of how I need to reflect God, just as the moon reflects the sun. I was motivated to take a walk through my neighborhood. I knew I was protected and had nothing to fear. As I walked, my kundalini energy rose, my clairvoyance increased, and my spiritual knowing was opened. I felt the cells of my body merge with the cells of everything around me. I felt, knew, and saw the people, houses, trees, even the asphalt around me. I experienced a oneness with everything.

I walked to a park and began to walk around the park. At the beginning of the walk, it was dark and I became afraid. I realized this represented the beginning of my spiritual path. As I continued to walk, it became lighter as light fell from some street lights and my fear disappeared; I realized that this represented my spiritual development and faith. I continued the walk around the park, and it became lighter and brighter as I walked. Some of the light was physical and some was spiritual light. I knew that this related to my life and my spiritual path, that as I continued on my path and stayed faithful to my calling, there would be more and more light in my life.

It was an ecstatic experience. The joy was amazing. I saw the spiritual guides helping me and experienced my oneness as spirit. I felt my body as a part of the physical world. I heard the spirits singing, saw the colors of spirit, and had the joy of feeling at one with God. I laughed on my way home as I realized why I had previously created this kind of experience in the wilderness. Asphalt is not as pleasant to be at one with as are rocks, dirt, and trees. This experience, like many others, is difficult to describe, but I am sure most people have had what they would describe as a spiritual experience or even as an ecstatic experience. The simplicity of the spiritual realm often keeps people from validating the power of their experience as they are expecting something complex.

Most experiences of ecstasy last a few minutes or a few hours. Some experiences last longer. The longest undisturbed period of time I experienced spiritual ecstasy lasted for ten days. My husband and I were on vacation in Eastern Washington in September. The weather was warm and the air was velvety soft. The clear skies provided amazing views of the stars at night and of the bluffs and distant vistas during the day. I had been aware, before we went on this vacation, of a special time that would be provided for me because I was starting the first book, on meditation, in the Key series of books.

The day after we arrived, I was meditating and my spiritual guides told me that I would have ten days of protection from the physical world. I also received this communication from my higher self, from the Archangel Michael, and Jesus. I knew this was to be a very special time for me since so many powerful sources told me about it. I accepted the information, but had no idea what it meant. I was told when the clear period would begin and end. On the appointed day, I felt such a drastic shift in my sense of reality that I could not deny the change in my relationship with the world. Everything was beautiful. My physical senses were heightened, yet I was detached from the physical world. My communication with the spiritual world was clearer and more real than my communication with the physical world. Fortunately, my husband was the only person I was relating to at the time.

This ten day period included a great deal of meditation, communication with spirit, and walking alone in the desert. My communication with God was constant. At night I spent many hours under the stars "talking" with various spiritual guidance. This time of healing and love prepared me and my body to write spiritual books over the next few years. The things I accomplished in the following years would not have been possible without this time of spiritual communion. To me, it was a time of ecstasy.

I learned that one can experience spiritual ecstasy and perform mundane tasks at the same time; that communication with God can be constant and uninterrupted when one is in a spiritual state; that there is an unlimited amount of spiritual help and guidance for everyone. I learned so much it will take me many years to make it manifest in my physical world through teaching and writing books. When the ten days were over, it was as drastic a change as when it began. I had no idea how much I was inundated by the physical world until I experienced being protected from it and then re-entered it. My challenge was to accept my mission in the physical world and not resist it after experiencing such joy and peace.

Some souls stay in a state of ecstasy instead of relating to the physical realm, but this is not my path. I had to return to the physical world to bring what I had learned into the awareness of those living in the material reality. It was a shock, at first, but I soon regained my perspective of my purpose and returned to enjoying my work in the material world. After all, I did still have friends, laughter, food, wine, sex, and other fun physical things to enjoy as well as the joy of my spiritual work.

Many people I have assisted in their spiritual awakening have told me about their experiences of ecstasy. When one student first learned about his kundalini energy and used it consciously, he said, "I feel like God when I run this energy." Many students in the class agreed they were experiencing a state of ecstasy as they raised their vibration and brought more energy into their physical bodies. Some of the students were busy focusing on clearing their fear of the power they felt flowing through them, or the pain the energy stimulated. All of the students in that class were aware of the power of the kundalini regardless of how it affected them. They were also aware of rapid change occurring in their physical system.

Spiritual awareness comes in stages and requires change. You must change to heal and grow. Kundalini energy creates rapid change. You grow spiritually just as you grow physically, in degrees. As you grow and mature spiritually, what you believe today may appear childish to you a year from today. This means you need to stop judging your process so you can continue to grow. When you accept yourself as you are, you can change and grow.

Humility is required when you use kundalini energy, so you can look at the "you" now and not judge the "you" of the past. You often change so rapidly you are amazed by your behavior or beliefs of only a few months past. I believe we receive information on a need-to-know basis and we hear what we are prepared to hear. Each change allows us to change and grow more. Spiritual ecstasy can be as simple and powerful as creating change in our belief system or as joyous as experiencing the beauty of nature, when we surrender to the process and allow the humility needed to be part of the whole.

Many of the stories about discovering and using kundalini energy and having experiences of ecstasy remind me of the transformation of a pupa in a cocoon into a butterfly in the air. People move from being limited by their body to being a free spirit with a body. It is a transformation from imprisonment to freedom. Spiritual freedom is the realization that the soul can create whatever it desires and believes, and that all things are possible. It is the realization that you are spirit and the body is your creation through which you communicate and create in the material world. Spiritual ecstasy is the experience of waking up to yourself as spirit, the revelation that you are a part of God, and knowing, seeing, and feeling this revelation.

"There is so much to know about yourself. Fortunately, learning about yourself is the most fascinating thing there is to do."

KUNDALINI AND THE HUMAN BODY

The human body is a spiritual creation. Spirit creates in matter to communicate, experience, create and learn. Spirit is a part of the Cosmic Consciousness. Spirit creates the illusion of separation from the Whole to isolate an aspect of its consciousness. That aspect can be developed and its energies and abilities increased in order to return what it gains to the Whole. The Earth and the human body are what we use to create a separate, creative space. A simple analogy of spirit separating from the Whole to create in matter is that of a father sending his son out into the world to learn and mature so the son can bring his talents back to assist the family. This is a physical explanation to help the intellect comprehend the spiritual creative process.

The planets, stars, and all material things are a spiritual creation. All of the physical creations are spiritual energy slowed down to manifest in the material world. What we call God created the planets, stars, and other celestial bodies of this universe and every other particle of the entirety of creation. We, as "children of God," create a body on a planet to express our spiritual creativity and learn more about creating. A soul is not given a planet to administer until it has learned to master a human body, so it is futile to attempt to skip spiritual steps. Learning to master a human body is a major lesson. It includes mastering the emotions, sexuality, intellect, body responses, survival instinct, reflexes, autonomic responses, and so forth. The soul has to learn how to control every aspect of the body and how to communicate and create through the body. Learning to know self is more than most people realize.

The human body is a composite of the soul's information and concepts, so the soul is learning to take control of its own creativity. The body is a composite of pictures, formulas, symbols, beliefs, and concepts that the soul has created over its many lifetimes, accepted from other souls, and created in the present life. The body is created according to the needs of the spiritual group called human beings here on planet Earth. We have agreed that we need the intelligence, body posture, and other evolutionary developments of the human body. The body is also created according to what the individual soul needs to learn within a particular life, with characteristics such as the gender, size, and genetic makeup. All bodies have the characteristics of operating in time and space, effort, and the other attributes described in the previous chapter.

The human body is the individual soul's personal

planet. Within its own space, the soul is like God and is the creator within the body. The soul is the creator of the body and of every bodily experience and creation through the body. The soul determines every aspect of the body including its gender, health, appearance, and size. It also creates the experiences and relationships it has in the body such as the parents, mate, children, work, talents, weaknesses, and strengths. If the soul has forgotten its spiritual nature, it functions completely on physical terms. If the soul is aware of itself, it creates with a spiritual perspective.

The soul learns how to come into a body, and then must learn how to get its energy out of the body and the material world, to return its energy to spiritual form. Kundalini energy is a major factor in this process of entering and leaving the body. Kundalini energy is important in the transformation of the spirit into and out of the human body. Kundalini energy raises the material level to the spiritual level so the soul can fully use the body while in it, and eventually take its energy out of the body and back into the spiritual realm.

A newborn friend of mine had some confusion about how to use his kundalini energy when he first arrived in his body. I was blessed to be at the birth of this friend, and like many souls, he made his entry in the middle of the night. The next day, I was taking a nap in the afternoon since I had been awake the night before. His parents called me and were frantic about the baby. He had a fever and had not defecated as newborn babies must do within a certain period of time. His parents were afraid they would have to take him to the hospital and get complex and painful medical help for him. I assured them that I would give the baby a healing. I laid back down for my nap, and, instead of sleeping, I communicated with the baby. I told him that he had to defecate and that he needed to turn down his kundalini energy. He had not been in a physical body for a long time. He had forgotten that you need to defecate to clean the physical system and that kundalini energy was not all that was needed for the job. The excess kundalini energy was causing the fever and the lack of focus on the need for physical cleansing.

I was just falling asleep when the parents called me back about twenty minutes later. The baby had defecated, and it was the most wonderful thing in the world. His temperature had gone back to normal, and they did not have to take him to the hospital. The parents were overjoyed as their baby was fine and healthy again. Both of these people are spiritually aware but had no interest in the spiritual aspect of this experience since the survival of the baby was their only concern. New parents are a great deal of fun to watch.

The baby knew about kundalini energy but had to remember about physical systems. One reason we have parents is to remind us how to work the physical systems called bodies. Kundalini helps the soul enter the body and fill it with his spiritual energy. The soul also needs to consider the way this physical system works. The body eats, sleeps, and eliminates, and the soul needs to keep it in proper working order. Like my baby friend, we need to balance spirit and body as we use kundalini energy.

If the soul is taught about its kundalini energy, it can use it during his or her entire life. However, most people are not informed about this energy, so they fill their body with inappropriate energies such as fear, hate, and pain to make the body feel real to them. They then create their physical world through these disturbing concepts instead of from spiritual energies. If the baby had gone to the hospital for a spinal tap, he would have had the experience of pain, fear, and confusion to create within until he cleared that memory. Instead, he adjusted his energies and created as spirit without trauma.

Kundalini energy increases the vibration in the body so the soul can clear what is not appropriate and fill the physical space with its spiritual energy. This high vibration can be disturbing if it is not understood. The spirit may have stored pain in its body, and kundalini energy will bring the pain to the surface and eventually cleanse it from the body. It is not as easy to be spiritually focused when the body is in pain, fear, or some other disturbing state of being as it is when the body is free of disturbance. The soul can use kundalini energy to transform the body into a more useful vehicle by cleansing inappropriate energies, but may pass through times of confusion and disturbance in the cleansing process.

Spirit creates a body to function in the material world. In the process, most souls forget that they are spirit by the time they are three or four years old. The material world engulfs the soul with the focus on survival, and there is not much education about the reality of spirit. The spontaneous experience of kundalini is often the factor that reawakens the soul to itself. In many Eastern societies, this is validated. In most Western cultures, there is such an intellectual focus on life that a kundalini experience is often interpreted as a physical or psychological illness or problem, instead of a spiritual experience.

Kundalini energy has a major impact on the physical body. This effect needs to be understood so you do not become afraid of your spiritual experiences. Knowing about kundalini energy also helps you control this energy instead of letting the kundalini energy control you. Kundalini energy, like all energies, can be consciously used in a controlled manner to create a desired experience. You do not have to wait for the kundalini energy to rise, but can consciously cause it to rise through the system. You can also turn off kundalini energy whenever you wish. You can be in control. Kundalini energy may frighten you if you are not aware of your spiritual nature and believe you are just your body. Thus, you need a spiritual focus and perspective to use kundalini energy safely.

The kundalini energy rising through the physical body can create a dramatic physical experience. The energy stimulates your entire energy system including all of the chakras and your trancemediumship. Trancemediumship is a system for spiritual communication. It can be used to increase communication between you and your body, and you and God. Trancemediumship can be used to raise your energy enough to leave the body and allow another spirit to enter and use the body for its communication through your body. Variations of trancemediumship are automatic writing and speaking in tongues. You can learn to control and use your trancemediumship to communicate as spirit without being invaded by other spirits. Since kundalini energy raises your energy and stimulates the chakras and the trancemedium abilities, you need to be aware and in control of your system so you do not get invaded and misguided. I suggest using your chakras, trancemediumship, and kundalini energy to turn within to yourself and God. You do not need to channel any energy except your own to experience God.

When using kundalini energy, whatever you have in your body and system will be stimulated and will come to the surface of your awareness. A young woman who was a student of martial arts and spiritual information had an adverse kundalini experience because she would not accept that she was having a spiritual experience. She wanted to relate her experience to the physical world only, and thus became disturbed, violent, and created a great deal of trouble for herself. Her kundalini energy moved through her system without her conscious control of it and stimulated her trancemediumship and past painful experiences stored in her chakras. She knew something was happening that she did not understand and went to see a teacher she trusted who lived in another city. On her way, she lost control of her body and was violent enough to be arrested and put in jail.

Fortunately, her spiritual community was informed about her situation and came to her assistance. She was released from jail and went to live with community members until her mother was able to take her to her home for a time of recuperation. Because of her violent behavior, she was required by authorities to go on drug therapy to help her deal with her energy. After several months with her family, she returned to her own home and attempted to continue her life. She was able to function until she again turned up her kundalini energy to a level where the powerful flow of energy caused her to stimulate her trancemediumship and bring up old pains and fears. She believed that the world was against her, so she did not trust anyone. She confused past and present and talked as if people in the present were doing things she had obviously seen and experienced earlier in her life. She again became violent and abusive, and was hospitalized. Her spiritual community and family were unable to reach her during this time as she refused to see, believe, or trust them.

Evidently this woman witnessed a rape and had been raped herself when she was a small child, but she had buried that experience so deeply in her subconscious that she did not have a conscious memory of the event. The rape had been done by men she depended on and trusted. When the kundalini energy brought the event to her conscious awareness, she was unable to deal with it and responded like the child she once was instead of like the woman she had become. The kundalini energy was rising in her body, and the pain and disturbance stored in her body was being stimulated and cleared. She refused to believe that she was experiencing a cleansing of her painful past and steadfastly clung to the belief that she was experiencing these events in the present. People continued to send her healings in hopes that she would awaken to her spiritual abilities and regain control of her system and life. This young woman lost control to the point that she killed herself. This story can help others be aware of how powerful kundalini energy is. This young woman did not die in vain if even one other person learns from her experience. I know of many, in fact, who learned from this experience about the power of kundalini energy in spiritual awakening, and the need to be aware and in control of one's healing process.

Kundalini energy can easily be misunderstood, misinterpreted, and misused. All of this can lead to physical disorders. Many people who are believed to have a physical problem actually are having a kundalini experience. Whether the problem is considered physical or psychological, it could be caused by the flow of kundalini energy and the resulting cleansing process. A person may have subconscious memories which are disturbing, and the emergence of these memories could create trauma in the system if he or she is not aware of what is happening. If the emerging experiences are disturbing enough, even a spiritually aware person is challenged to deal with the emotions being stimulated. Freud discovered, through hypnosis, that people have memories buried in their subconscious. These subconscious memories can cause inappropriate behavior in the present when they are stimulated in some way.

The subconscious memories are a main reason why it is important to begin meditating and learning to control your energy before you turn on your kundalini energy, since kundalini stimulates these subconscious memories. If you are grounded and in control of your energetic system when a major change occurs, you can maintain your control. If you are not grounded and in charge of your system, any change that happens is disturbing and a major awakening can seem catastrophic. Taking responsibility for your body and the reality you have created through that body is essential to effectively deal with your kundalini energy.

Personal responsibility is very important in the physical world and in the spiritual realm as well. You need to be responsible for whatever you have created in your reality whether it is witnessing the disturbing behavior of others or remembering your own behavior. You, as spirit, may have asked to know the truth about someone and been given the opportunity to see their true nature instead of what they project to the world. If you do not own that you wanted this truth, then you will be in denial of a major experience in your life. Denial keeps you from being in charge of your energy and causes you to create through fear. To be in charge, you have to be responsible for yourself.

Kundalini energy is the transformer. It transforms the physical to the spiritual. It changes energy tied up in physical vibrations such as fear and pain into powerful, neutral spiritual energy. It changes heavy to light, murky to clear, disturbing to joyous, fear to calm, and every other physical energy or disruption to spiritual energy and even enlightenment. Regardless of what we have created in our physical system, we can transform it back into spiritual energy. Kundalini energy changes energy invested in mental image pictures, concepts, or symbols back into pure energy. This power can create trauma or joy, depending on what we are transforming and how much we take responsibility for our creativity. Our personal responsibility helps us use kundalini energy with ease and awareness.

Spiritual transformation is a powerful experience and kundalini energy is a powerful force. As you cleanse and transform your body into the vehicle it is meant to be, it becomes your friend and not your enemy. Your body will become healthier and desire things that make it healthy such as exercise, clean air, water, and healthy food. It may pass through stages of disturbance and unhealthy habits in its process of cleansing, but the body's focus will eventually become health and well-being.

Kundalini energy affects the body more than any other single energy. It can transform your body and your relationship to your body and your other physical creations. It is worth the challenge of learning how to control and use kundalini energy because it is a powerful healing vibration. Like any power, kundalini energy must be used with care and respect. Kundalini energy can change your life. It is up to you how you change.

PHYSICAL RESPONSES TO KUNDALINI ENERGY

Kundalini energy can cause many different reactions in the physical body. Some of the body's reactions to kundalini are pleasant and some of them are not. The body's response depends on how you have treated your body and what you have stored in it. Everyone knows how they have treated their body, so it is easy to determine how to approach the use of kundalini energy. If you have abused your body with drugs, overeating, tension, lack of sleep or exercise, or any of the other million and one ways people abuse their bodies, then you have cleaning work to do before your experiences will be the ecstasy you seek.

No one is perfect. We all have bad habits and unhealthy life patterns. We can turn on and use our kundalini energy regardless of the state of the body, but we need to be aware that the body will respond according to its present state of being. If the body contains fear, it will experience this emotion as the kundalini moves through the system since kundalini energy stimulates whatever is in the body. The fear will be increased for a time as it is brought up and cleansed by the kundalini flow. If the process is blocked or resisted, the fear will remain prominent for as long as the kundalini flows and the interference exists.

The kundalini flow has to be allowed to cleanse and change whatever physical energy it stimulates, or it will magnify it instead. If you are clearing pain, the kundalini will wash it away without resistance, but if you resist, the pain will intensify. This confuses many people as they expect the kundalini process to happen instantly, regardless of what they do. In reality, you have to learn non-resistance and develop patience to allow your spiritual process. Instead of fighting your healing, you have to be willing to change.

Most people do not know how to relax and allow things to be as they are, thus they resist and struggle against their own healing process. People also have difficulty with patience. Patience is required since the physical body operates in time and space, and the healing that kundalini energy creates takes time. The kundalini energy is a powerful force, and once released, can become a problem if the person fights the cleansing instead of allowing it to happen through time. Like the young woman who fought her healing, it is easy to get caught in fighting yourself instead of allowing the transformation to occur.

Information can help you understand your kundalini

energy and how it affects you. Many common physical problems are actually caused by using kundalini energy improperly. If you use it correctly, it can be wonderful beyond description. If you use it incorrectly, it can be disturbing to the point of trauma. It is up to you how you use this transforming force. It is powerful, so it needs to be used gently, with common sense and personal responsibility.

We store information and energy throughout our bodies. Some of this is inappropriate energy, such as someone else's information, pain, fear, lies, hate, or other corrosive vibrations that interfere with the spirit's communication with the body and with God. We need present-time pain and fear as survival warning systems to keep the body alive, but we do not need to store past pain and fear experiences since we will continue to create through them. Kundalini energy hits any stored pain, fear, hate, or foreign energy when it begins to move. The stronger the flow, the stronger the reaction from the body as the energy hits the blockage.

Headaches are a common response of the body to kundalini energy being blocked or used improperly. The kundalini energy flows up the spine and out the top of the head, at the top of the spine. If you blast on your kundalini energy and have an energy block in your head, the kundalini energy will hit this foreign or inappropriate energy and can cause pain. If you use the kundalini energy gently, it can melt away the interference to its flow, and thus clear the disruptive energy. Once the block is cleared, the energy can flow freely.

I had several accidents as a child and stored many of those pain experiences or pictures in my head. If I ran my kundalini energy gently, it was comfortable; but, if I ran it strongly, I experienced a headache. When I learned how to cleanse these pain memories from the energy channels in my head, I was able to allow a stronger flow of kundalini energy. The gentle flow of kundalini energy helped clear the past pain and allowed more space in my head for my spiritual vibration. When I consciously started the healing process, the past pain would send me to the aspirin bottle and sometimes to bed. After years of healing work, I am able to quickly and easily clear the remaining old pain as it emerges, by running my kundalini energy gently through the area in pain.

My husband and I have had the experience of assisting many people heal their headaches. We have often cleared people's energy channels in their head, and the headache immediately disappeared. This seems like a miracle to someone who does not understand energy or does not have a spiritual perspective. It is simply the use of energy to open channels in the head so the kundalini energy can flow without interference. Once the interference is cleared, the kundalini energy can move freely to transform the disturbance to a higher vibration and eliminate the physical problem.

Another common response of the body to hitting

interference to the flow of kundalini energy is backaches. Since the main channel for kundalini energy is the spine, if there is any disruption to the flow of this high vibration in the spine, it will cause a block in the flow. This block will be similar to a dam in a stream; the energy will back up, overflow, or turn off. Any of these responses to the "dam" of energy can cause pain in the spine or the area of the body into which the kundalini energy overflows.

From a spiritual perspective, the spine is one of the most important parts of the physical body since it is the channel for the kundalini energy. If the spine is out of alignment, injured, filled with pain or other disturbing energies, then the kundalini process can be interrupted.

Think of your spine as a stream of vital energy flowing through your body, and you will begin to see the importance of your kundalini energy and of the channel through which it flows. The spine carries the nerves which connect the brain with all parts of the body, so without the spine, the body does not work. The spine contains the kundalini channels also, so this vital spiritual energy runs through the spine. Everyone can run kundalini energy, but most people do not run it correctly, often because of spinal problems. This may keep you from using as much of this dynamic energy as you would like to use. You may need to do some physical work to heal your spine if you are having difficulty with it. Once you have your spine healed, you can use your kundalini energy more effectively to heal your entire system. Your body does not need to be perfect or even healthy to use kundalini energy, but the process is easier if it is healthy.

Because of my childhood injuries, I have had to focus a great deal on healing my spine. I have used meditation, kundalini meditation, massage, tai chi, chiropractic, acupuncture, exercise, stretching, and yoga during my life. All of these healing techniques have helped me to re-own my spine and allow the power of kundalini energy which I need for my spiritual work in this life. I have learned that there are many ways to heal yourself and your body, and it is best to focus on the methods that work for you in the present. One phase in your development may require more physical focus and another phase may take you into yourself with a deeper spiritual focus. It is necessary to be in touch with yourself in the present and with what you need to fulfill your spiritual goals.

Meditating on your spine helps you discover what you need to do to heal it and use it as the channel for your kundalini energy. If your spine is in pain, you need to focus on clearing the pain. If you do not own your spine, you will need to own it before you can use it fully. The kundalini energy needs a clear channel and the spine contains that channel. If your spine is filled with foreign or inappropriate energy, that is what you need to deal with when you turn on your kundalini energy. You may have backaches before you have ecstasy.

Kundalini energy affects the body in many ways. It often raises the temperature of the physical body. It is like a powerful thermal current. Your body may respond with a flushed or splotchy red face. You may feel heat moving up your spine. You can quickly become hot and sweaty. The body may have hot flashes. The menopausal symptom of hot flashes is caused partly by the emergence of kundalini energy in the older female body. Since the older female body is changing from being a creator of babies to being more spiritually focused, the transforming kundalini energy is part of this process. Many of the symptoms attributed to menopause are actually the body's response to kundalini energy as the body transforms from being a physical creator to a spiritual creator. "Hot flashes" may already be a familiar experience for a woman or man who has consciously used his or her kundalini energy earlier in life. The hormonal changes, for a women, may not be as disturbing if the kundalini energy is understood and controlled. I have experienced this phenomenon all of my life.

This increased heat in the body caused by kundalini energy flowing through the system causes other interesting phenomena. The body can become so hot that it perspires profusely or is hot to the touch. This often occurs when the body is asleep. The experience of "night sweats" can be caused by running a great deal of kundalini energy while asleep. Many people experience their kundalini while sleeping as their intellect and other physical responses do not interfere at this time.

A student came to me asking to talk about a personal problem that her doctor could not explain. She was embarrassed because she would wake up in the middle of the night and her sheets would be wet from her perspiration. When I explained that it was her kundalini energy flowing while she slept, she was relieved that it was something she could understand. She was still upset about the wet sheets as her new husband was not a spiritual student and wanted an intellectual explanation about what he considered a physical problem. I reminded her that she knew how to turn her kundalini energy down and off if she considered it necessary. She chose to turn her energy off, to accommodate her intellectual husband, and soon left her spiritual work. Fortunately, she had a baby soon after that, and the child helped her to reawaken spiritually. She is not as easily embarrassed about bodies now that she has two children, so she is more accepting of her own body and its responses to her spiritual growth.

My husband calls me his little furnace. At night, while I sleep, my body becomes so heated that he says it is uncomfortable to touch. I have always used my time of sleep to do a great deal of spiritual work outside of the body, and my kundalini energy flowing through the body helps me do this. The more energy I can run through my physical body, the more I can accomplish in both the physical and astral planes. The astral body is part of this physical world and is the body we use while the physical body sleeps. The flow of kundalini energy increases the clarity of the astral body as well as the physical body and makes both bodies easier for spirit to use.[3]

Kundalini energy is helpful in every aspect of spiritual creativity and must be respected because of its power. It transforms what we have invested in the physical world back into spiritual energy. Unfortunately, most people have not been taught about this energy or how to use it. The lack of understanding causes confusion and a fear of kundalini energy. There are many physical illnesses that cannot be diagnosed which, in fact, are caused by the lack of understanding and the misuse of kundalini energy. One common problem is rashes. There are many skin rashes that do not have a physical explanation. Some of these unexplainable rashes even have names because they are so common, but no one has an explanation for the cause. Many of these rashes are caused by kundalini energy running incorrectly.

If there is an energy blockage in the spine and the kundalini energy is flowing strongly, the kundalini energy will be interrupted and will flow outside of its proper channels. When this happens, a rash can occur on the skin indicating the irritation caused by the kundalini energy's "eruption". Skin rashes are not all caused by kundalini energy, but if you have one that is unexplainable, you may want to make sure your kundalini energy is flowing properly.

I recently taught a kundalini class after not teaching

kundalini classes for over a year. When a group of people put their attention on this energy and run the energy together, this can have an impact on people who associate with the members of the group, even if they are not in the class. After two weeks, several members of the community came to me individually complaining about an unexplainable rash. I laughed, since most of the complaints came from the staff. I saw that they were matching the energy of the kundalini class. When they put their attention on their own kundalini energy flow, as individuals, and cleared the spine, they healed their mysterious rash within a few hours or a few days.

Kundalini energy is wonderful to work with when you know what you are doing. It can be frightening to experience the body's response to it if you do not know what is happening. This is an important energy to know about and a major enhancer of personal healing. Learning to talk to your body is a helpful way to overcome your body's fears. If you have a clear communication with your body, you can learn what is happening with it and what you, as spirit, need to do about it. You will know if you need a spiritual, or a physical solution, or a combination of both. If your kundalini energy is not moving correctly, you may need to meditate and to stretch and exercise. Yoga is a system of postures, stretches, and exercises to enhance the flow of kundalini energy through the body. When you work with your body, and use it correctly, you find it easy to create what you, as spirit, are here to do.

The body communicates mainly with emotions. When you turn on your kundalini energy, your body responds with emotions. Kundalini helps you stimulate the body's emotional state and bring it into your conscious awareness. It does not allow you to deny your emotions since it brings them up and out. You may frighten yourself and others if your emotions emerge fast and furiously. The more you deny your emotions, the more strongly they will emerge. I once had the experience of laughing more than others thought appropriate. I meditated on the experience and saw how much I had been repressing my amusement to make others feel comfortable. I quickly started a healing process to allow my amusement and joy.

While running kundalini energy, if the body expresses fear, you may be clearing old fears from the body or the body may be afraid of its own death. It is easier to clear past fears than it is to gain seniority over the body's fear of death. Running kundalini energy helps you bring more of your spiritual energy into your body. This communicates your immortality as spirit to your body, and your body becomes more aware of its own mortality. The most important thing to your body is to stay alive, thus when it begins to be conscious of your immortality and its mortality, it has to face the issues of physical death. This usually causes the body to be afraid until you, the spirit, gain greater seniority with your body by moving the body's vibration above the level of fear and destroying any lies you have about death.

This fear of death is a major disturbance for people beginning to use their kundalini energy. Many people are not aware of themselves as spirit and as their spiritual energy comes into their physical consciousness, it is both exciting and frightening. Fear can be beneficial for survival with the fight or flight instinct, but can become detrimental if stored from the past or projected into the future. Fear can become a dominant emotion if the body gets focused on its survival and its fear of death while awakening the system. The spirit can overcome this fear of death, but it requires a spiritual focus and a determination to gain spiritual seniority with the body. Fear is a powerful and disturbing emotion, so it takes time and attention to gain control of it.

Even spiritually aware souls can get caught in the body's fear of death while awakening the consciousness. Fear of death can be overwhelming if the soul does not acknowledge the natural survival focus of its body. By being aware of the immortality of spirit and the mortality of the body, the soul can learn to work with its body to bring in more spiritual energy and help the body overcome its fear of death. This process takes time and attention and is part of what Jesus Christ, and all the great teachers, meant by "overcoming death."

My husband has gained a great deal of seniority with death and the fear of death. He started his growth process at age six when his mother died in a car wreck while he was sitting on her lap. He continued to create growth to gain seniority by being a medic in World War II where he saw a great deal of suffering and death. When he had a heart attack many years ago, he displayed his seniority with his body. I was afraid, and he looked at me and quietly said, "Honey, I'm not dying." I felt reassured, relieved, and awed and have focused on gaining seniority on this level ever since.

You do not become emotionally cold or unfeeling about death or dying by using your kundalini to become senior to death. You can become compassionate and understanding by learning to be in control of your own emotions. You can learn to see the spiritual aspect of death and learn to control the body's fear of death. Birth and death are similar for spirit as they are both spiritual transitions. Birth transitions the soul into a body and death is the spiritual transition out of a body. Kundalini energy can help you gain this spiritual seniority, but you may pass through fear on your journey.

Often the emotions that arise when the kundalini energy is moving through the system come from past experiences. Patience and continued focus on the cleansing process move these past-time emotions and experiences from the body. If the emotions relate to a present-time creation, the kundalini energy can be a great help in moving the emotion through the body. For example, if someone is in a rage, kundalini energy can help move the rage up and out of the body so the soul can regain control of the body and its emotions. The power of the kundalini energy may frighten the body as it moves the emotion and makes the emotion feel stronger than before until it diminishes or moves out of the system.

A woman who was a student of mine several years ago had a problem with her fury. She was sexually abused by her father as a child. She became a prostitute as a young woman because she believed that she had to do what men told her to do. She grew to hate herself and did not understand why she acted as she did. She was intelligent, educated, and beautiful and did not financially need to be a prostitute. She discovered her buried childhood experiences and the answers to her questions through meditation.

Once she awakened her subconscious memory, she was furious with her parents. She was not able to control her level of rage and became afraid of its power over her. She learned how to run her kundalini energy, and by focusing it on moving and clearing her fury, she was able to gain control of it. She eventually learned to control her anger and to use it in her healing process. She gained seniority with her emotions and began creating on a spiritual level. She is now healing herself instead of fighting her past. She is married and creating a business with her husband.

Another physical response to kundalini energy is the experience of feeling isolated. Many people experience a state of paranoia or feel that everyone is against them when they turn on their kundalini energy. This can be caused by the kundalini energy stimulating past experiences of being hurt and not having anyone to help. It can also be the experience of feeling very different from everyone else, and thus alone. Kundalini energy is a powerful flow of energy and gives the person a new awareness of the world within and around him. Kundalini energy flowing does separate him from the physical focus. If the person is tuned into the world around him, he will be focused on others when the kundalini moves through his system and will feel isolated from his surroundings as he is different. This can be especially disturbing if these other people are not spiritually focused. For example, if you are at a party and your kundalini energy turns on, you may begin to see colors around the guests and sounds may become louder; you may then feel separate from everyone; you could become afraid of the people and the experience and feel isolated in the middle of the party.

The kundalini energy stimulates the spiritual ability of clairvoyance or clear seeing. If the people around you are not open and honest souls, you will see their facades, protections, and lies and may become afraid of their falsehoods. These people may not be aware of their own facades and lies if they are not spiritually aware. You may feel disturbed if you are seeing these people clearly for the first time. Since most people have something they want to hide or lie about, it is easy to feel that others are against you when you begin to see clearly. Many people do not want to be seen clearly.

This state of feeling that everyone is against you can be overcome by continuing to meditate with your kundalini energy. You will eventually turn within to your personal system and begin to clear your own lies and facades and be able to accept others as they are. When you accept yourself as you are, you can see others as they are, without fear. Kundalini energy helps your clairvoyance turn on and helps you clear the body of the fear of what you are seeing. People may be opposed to you becoming more spiritually aware and in charge, but you will not be afraid of their beliefs once you become aware of the power of your own energy and beliefs.

A sense of your own power may lead you to another state of being that is common when you first turn on your kundalini. The feeling of being invincible is a common experience at the beginning of using kundalini energy. Like the student said, "I feel like God when I run this energy." This is known intellectually as a delusion of grandeur. It is a realization of the fact that you are spirit and a part of God. This is a major awakening, and the spiritual awareness you experience can allow you to accept the aspect of God within you. It is a problem only if you believe you are special and do not see that everyone is a part of God.

Once you have learned to accept that you are spirit,

you can settle down to the cleansing work you need to do to manifest your spirituality in your physical world. The state of feeling invincible or grand passes as you continue to use your kundalini energy because you eventually see that everyone is spirit and a part of God. A student once said to me, "I finally figured it out. I'm special!" "That is right," I answered, "and so is everyone else." She pouted, "I don't like that part." Unfortunately, this student did not continue her growth and chose to stay in the state of "feeling special." She lost her spiritual path, and the last time I heard of her, she was not doing well spiritually or physically.

There is great joy in seeing that we are spirit and a part of God. We also need to realize that we are a part of the Whole and not the totality of God. Many people awaken to their spiritual nature and end up losing themselves because they get caught in what I call the "God complex." When a soul believes it is special in the awareness of God or special compared to other souls or more powerful than others or superior in any way, then that soul has lost its spiritual perspective and is operating from the body's perspective of physical survival.

Viewing life as good, better, best is a physical perspective and does not relate to spiritual reality. The Cosmic Consciousness does not rate souls the way we grade students. In sports, someone may be the champion for awhile, but eventually someone else will come along who is better. This is the physical world of competition and survival of the fittest. The spiritual realm is not like the physical. Spiritual awareness eventually brings the realization that we are all One, and each part is meant to be itself for the Whole to function best. We are similar to a body where the eye is as important as the foot. Unfortunately, we often get caught in the competition levels of the body and try to superimpose this on our spiritual creativity.

If your kundalini energy stimulates this level of competition or one-upsmanship in you, you may have the experience of believing you are superior to others. You may experience a time of avoidance and denial. Eventually, you will have to face your lack of self-worth, pain, and other inappropriate energies that are the basis for your ego games. If you do see yourself as you are, instead of how you wish to be, you will realize that you are spirit and a part of God. This realization is worthy of great joy and celebration. If you continue to mature, you will also rejoice in the spirituality of all things. As it says in the Judeo-Christian Bible, "For He maketh His sun to rise on the evil and on the good, and sendeth rain on the just and on the unjust." We are all part of God, even the people we do not like.

The ego is a challenge for every soul to face when in a human body. There is always a temptation to create facades, protections, and other lies to pretend that we are what we believe others want us to be or what we expect ourselves to be. We are all challenged to release our ego levels as we become aware as spirit. The kundalini energy can stimulate the ego as it cleanses the system, and, in the process, we can get caught in believing the lies we have created. If we have a belief that we are special and the kundalini energy stimulates this concept, we can get caught believing this lie instead of letting it go. When the kundalini energy brings up an ego level, it may be more difficult to release than pain or fear as it appears to be attractive and validating. In reality, if we try to operate from the ego level, it will eventually cause pain and fear in the body as the ego is a lie, and we cannot live a lie without experiencing disturbance.

Kundalini energy is an effective cleanser for ego problems. Kundalini energy is a powerful, no-effort flow of energy that overrides the intellect. The ego is tied in with the intellect, so it is difficult to clear from an intellectual perspective. In fact, it can take years to discover some ego levels if they have been part of the system for a long time as they appear to be part of the body. Kundalini energy easily transforms physical energy back to a spiritual state, even the ego levels into which we invest so much of our energy. The more the ego is transformed, the more one's spiritual nature and light are able to shine through the body and other physical creations.

Kundalini energy can also easily stimulate states of being which are euphoric. This euphoric state can be experienced by anyone who turns on kundalini energy in any way. The experience may last a short time or an extended period of time. The growth that may result from this state can be less than euphoric, however, and this confuses people as they expect the euphoria to last forever. Anyone who has experienced a state of euphoria does not forget it and sometimes tries to recreate the experience through physical avenues, such as using drugs.

People turn on their kundalini energy in many ways without realizing what they are doing, so they do not know how to make it happen again. Music, dance, sex, drugs, religious fervor, strenuous exercise, childbirth, and other high energy experiences can trigger the flow of a person's kundalini energy. Many of the phenomena attributed to these experiences are actually the result of the kundalini energy flowing. This energy can cause the person to feel uplifted, euphoric, and in an altered state of consciousness. It can also frighten someone if that person is afraid of power or unusual experiences or is stimulating internal disturbance.

People are particularly open to kundalini experiences during puberty since the physical body is already in a state of transformation from childhood to adulthood. When I was twelve, I attended a large religious conference where the energy was high. During the main meeting, I experienced heat flowing through my body, a heightened sense of myself and my body, and an awakening of something within myself. I felt euphoric to the point of having tears stream down my cheeks. I knew my experience was not the religious fervor that some people have during religious meetings, but I did not know how to explain my experience. I did know that something wonderful had happened to me. It was years before I realized that my kundalini energy had turned on and opened up my chakras or energy centers. Fortunately, I did not create any damage to my system or become enamored with the conference speaker.

The experience of "falling in love" usually involves the flow of kundalini energy. Our system is awakened by the vibration of love and by sexual energy, and then the kundalini energy turns on, creating warmth, tingling, and a sense of euphoria. Kundalini can cause the person to feel light-headed and have a sense of walking on air. If people knew that some of their experience was kundalini energy when they "fell in love," maybe they could be more neutral about their experience. Many of the symptoms of "falling in love" are experiences of kundalini energy rising.

Someone else can turn on or stimulate your kundalini energy. This can occur unconsciously, or someone may consciously stimulate this energy in your space. You need to be aware if someone affects you in this way so you can avoid any power games. Unfortunately, some people who learn about the power of kundalini energy use their knowledge to manipulate others. Anyone who uses their abilities and energies to manipulate other people is not spiritually focused since a spiritual focus is an inward focus. You do not need to give up seniority to another person about your kundalini energy. You are able to turn it on and off and to run it your way. You can take charge of your energy by owning and taking responsibility for it. You are not being responsible for yourself if you give up control of your system to someone else.

Most people have had a kundalini experience at some time in their life. Whether it was frightening or euphoric, the experience was probably unforgettable. Whether the experience was ecstatic or disturbing, the power of it made an impression. The flow of kundalini energy always gets some response from the physical body. The more one uses this energy, the more adjusted the body becomes to the flow of kundalini. The body responds less drastically as it cleanses and adjusts to the kundalini vibration and the resulting physical changes. Kundalini energy can become a constant part of one's life experience.

The kundalini energy is easy to consciously turn on and off. Very few people know how to do this, so it remains a mystery instead of becoming a natural part of one's creative experience. It is time for people to wake up to their spiritual nature and to how their spiritual vibrations affect their body and other creations. The kundalini energy is one of the most dramatic spiritual energies that we use, and this energy needs to be de-mystified so people can begin to use it consciously without fear.

We can transform the heaviness and effort of our physical existence to a lightness and ease by using our kundalini energy in a conscious manner. The body can become a lighter vibration which makes it easier for us, as spirit, to flow through it. Spirit is here to learn about creativity, and the body is its main creative vehicle. Kundalini energy is a vibration to transform the physical creation of the body to a higher vibration for spiritual use. All of the spiritual teachers used this vibration to spiritualize their bodies so they could bring their high spiritual vibration into the physical body. Not everyone is supposed to be a spiritual teacher, but everyone can learn to use kundalini energy in a safe way to increase his or her spiritual manifestation on Earth.

You can begin the process by learning to know your body. Pay attention to your body, its responses to you, and what you create, and you will begin a dialogue that will help you, as spirit, regain control of your body. Since the kundalini process affects the body, it is important for you to know your body so you can be in control of what happens within your body as it responds to the kundalini energy. The body is being transformed, so you need to understand your body in order to create what you want in the transformation process.

Meditation is an excellent way to learn about you, as spirit, and about your body and what you have created within it. If you attempt to avoid your body when you begin to use your kundalini energy, you will create discord in your system as the body is what is changing the most. Meditate on your communication and relationship with your body, and you will be better prepared to work with your body while using kundalini energy. If you do not talk to your body, your body may gain control and stop your kundalini energy and healing process. The body may also change the course of your spiritual awakening to a physical focus on survival issues such as power games, ego, or emotional games.

You may plan to use your kundalini energy to withdraw yourself from the physical world for spiritual work outside of your body. You may want to use your kundalini energy to help you move more into your body for a sport, your work, or to manifest your spiritual energy into your daily life. Whether you want to be removed from or more involved in the body, you are still using the body as a vehicle in the physical world. You cannot create on the same level if you do not have a body. The transformation of the body to a higher energy level requires communication with the body whether you are training the body to do without you or to deal more with you.

Your body is your vehicle and has a response to everything you create in or through it. It is necessary to deal with your body regardless of what you create in this world. Kundalini energy is a powerful energy that transforms the body to a higher vibration. You need to tell your body what you are doing so it will not turn off or redirect the process because it is afraid or confused. Your body can be fun to work with once you realize that you are spirit and not your body and that you create everything in your life.

Kundalini energy is wonderful. You and your body can benefit greatly by learning to use it consciously. Kundalini energy can transform your experience from the limits of a physical perspective of life to the revelation that you are spirit and a part of God. It can help you see that all of your creations are of a spiritual nature and that you have the power to create what you need. If you keep meditating and using your kundalini energy, you may even experience ecstasy.

Sexuality and Kundalini Energy

Sexual energy is a powerful energy that can be expressed in many ways. We must be conscious about how we wish to use this powerful energy when we turn on kundalini energy, as sexual energy can be stimulated and empowered by the kundalini energy.

We must remember that sex relates to a wide spectrum of experience from birth through life to death. We need to be aware that sexual energy has the power to create life and thus death, which is an end to physical life. This is a great power within an individual and an even greater power between two people. The main purpose of sexual energy is to impregnate to create a body for another soul to use.[4] This power needs to be used wisely and carefully.

Sexual energy is one of the most powerful survival aspects of the physical body. We are immortal spirit, but the survival of the physical species is dependent on human sexuality. Humans must procreate for the species to continue and for us to have physical vehicles to use. We forget that our sexuality is a survival drive for the body, since most of us are not living in small groups where everyone is dependent on the growth of the group for survival. We have veiled our human characteristics with technology and industry, but we still have our human nature. Whether we are living on a farm where many children are helpers or in a city apartment where children may seem a burden, we still have the drive to create new members for our "tribe." We have also forgotten the spiritual aspect of sexuality: that sex creates life and all that is involved in life.

The focus on sexuality in technological society is a socially acceptable way of acting out this survival drive and avoiding our spiritual responsibility. Most people no longer have tigers to fight to meet survival needs, so we often focus on our sexual nature to satisfy our body's survival drives. Technology and the industrial revolution have changed our outward lives so much that many people have forgotten how significant the survival drive is in all human actions, particularly the sexual energy. Modern society also ignores the responsibility we have for our powerful sexual energy.

The sexual nature of humans is a strong drive and is emphasized in present-time because there are so few other outlets for our survival nature, except in times of war, famine, or natural disasters, and because we have forgotten our spiritual nature. Often the sexual drive is confused with emotions and other communications from the body since there is so much attention on sexuality. Very few people acknowledge the spiritual aspect and power of sexual energy. Movies, television, books, magazines, and other forms of media use sex to sell their products and to draw attention to their shows without consideration of the survival or spiritual nature of sex. There is so much attention on this one aspect of our human survival drive that, in some societies, it is obsessive. Many people believe their reality is based on their sexuality. This has created many industries to help people remain young-looking and sexually appealing. This is a survival drive out of balance.

Sexuality is often confused with kundalini energy as it has some similar characteristics and effects on the body and because one often stimulates the other. Our spiritual development is confusing when we equate kundalini energy with our sexuality. Both sex and kundalini energy can make your face turn red, cause you to feel light-headed, make your body feel hot and tingly, and cause you to leave your body. Both sex and kundalini energy can stimulate an orgasmic release of energy and are great creative powers. The difference is that sex relates to the procreation of the species and its subsequent survival, and kundalini energy relates to the transformation of physical energy to a higher spiritual vibration. Sexual and kundalini energies flow through different channels in the spiritual system and relate to the physical body differently. Sexuality can stimulate kundalini energy and vice versa, but they are different vibrations with different purposes, flowing through different channels.

Since most societies are focused on sexuality, we can easily confuse these two powerful energies. Children are often taught that their kundalini energy is their sexual energy because their parents are ignorant of the existence of kundalini energy. If a child turns on her kundalini energy and her face turns red and she has a high energy, her mother may relate this to her sexuality. The mother may teach her daughter to be afraid of her kundalini energy believing it to be her sexual energy. She may tell her daughter that it is dangerous to use this energy as it might attract attention and harm. The girl could grow up being afraid of her kundalini energy and never gain control of it because she did not know what it was and associates kundalini with her sexuality.

If your parents were afraid of their own sexuality and confused kundalini energy with sexual energy, you may have some of the same concepts about kundalini that you have about your sexuality. If your parents were upset if you masturbated and they thought that was what you were doing when you ran kundalini energy, you could have a great deal of confusion about kundalini energy. You have to meditate on any misinformation about sexuality you received from your family or other teachers, and clear it. You also need to meditate on clearing any misinformation you have learned about your kundalini energy or confusion between sexuality and kundalini.

Kundalini energy is an energy of spiritual

transformation while sexual energy is primarily for the survival of the species. While both energies are powerful creative forces, the main purpose of kundalini is spiritual and the main purpose of sexuality is physical. This realization helps separate these energies in your awareness which helps you use each for its specific purpose. Meditation and the use of each of these energies on a conscious level can help you clearly see and feel the difference between the two vibrations. There are also other uses for both sexual and kundalini energies such as healing, communication, and raising the body's vibration; but, when you look at the main purpose of these energies, it is easy to see the difference.

Another reason people confuse kundalini and sexuality is the association of kundalini energy with celibacy. Kundalini energy helps transform any body energy into spiritual energy, even the strong vibration of sexuality. Anyone who wants to be celibate needs to learn how to run kundalini energy to release the sexual energy of the body. Celibacy is the choice to completely abstain from all sexual interactions. This can be a disturbing and even painful experience if the person does not know how to transform sexual energy into spiritual energy. Kundalini energy can be used to move the sexual energy up through the body transforming it for use on a spiritual level.

Many religions and societies require celibacy for various reasons. Societies may require celibacy for solidarity, the safety of the group, or for family planning.

Religions require celibacy for a variety of reasons from judging the body, to demanding spiritual seniority with the body. The spiritual purpose for celibacy is to gain seniority with the body, to the point the soul can use the powerful sexual energy of the body for a spiritual level. This requires discipline, commitment, and kundalini energy.

A young priest came to us years ago seeking information about kundalini energy. He heard that kundalini energy could help him be celibate and that we had information about kundalini energy. He was frantic when he first came to us as he was a sincere spiritual seeker and minister, but he was having great difficulty dealing with his sexual drive. He had the misfortune, for someone in his position, to be handsome and personable, which attracted the attention of many women in his church. He spent some time learning new techniques of meditation, and then learning about kundalini energy.

He claimed that the kundalini energy saved his calling as a priest because he was able to release the sexual tension through the flow of kundalini energy. He was amazed how much more energy he had when he used kundalini to transform his sexuality into spiritual energy. It is unfortunate that spiritual vocations which require celibacy do not teach about kundalini energy to assist in transforming the sexual energy for spiritual use. Physical energies can be transformed, but cannot be denied or ignored without creating a problem that will eventually erupt.

The transformation of sexual energy into spiritual energy can create a variety of experiences. The experience can even feel similar to an orgasm in the spine. It is more subtle, but as enjoyable and energizing. The release of sexual energy is not always as dramatic as the sensation of a spinal orgasm, but usually simply feels warm, tingly, or like any other energy being transformed. It is important to realize that sexual energy can be used for spiritual purposes, and we do not have to be controlled by this survival level of the body. It is also important to acknowledge sexual energy as a powerful creative force.

You do not have to become celibate or even diminish your sex life to use kundalini energy. Kundalini can help you take greater control of your sexuality and even to create a clearer, higher sexual energy. People often have their kundalini energy turned on during sex and experience this extra intensity of energy flow. Kundalini can help release pain and disturbance around sexuality so it can be healing and enjoyable. You need to evaluate your purpose for using either kundalini or sexual energies, as you are working with great creative power. The power increases tremendously when you use these energies together. Know yourself and your motives for using power.

A student had the problem of being an attractive man in a group of mostly women. He received so much sexual attention from the women, he was uncomfortable and even in pain. He asked me for help, and I taught him how to turn his kundalini energy on and off. He rapidly took control of his body by using his kundalini energy to release the sexual tension caused by the women invading his body space. He was delighted to know that he did not have to be a victim of other people's desires. This can also be true for women who experience their space being invaded by someone else's sexual desires.

Any time you feel overwhelmed by your sexual drive or another's sexual attention, you can use your kundalini energy to release the sexual tension and gain control of your body. There is no good or bad about your sexuality; it is a survival energy and creative power in the physical world. How you deal with your body determines how you create in this reality. If you are here to create a large family, or to be sexually active in any manner, you may want to express your sexuality a great deal. If on the other extreme, you are in a body to create a spiritual focus, then the kundalini energy is of great assistance in transforming your sexual energy for your spiritual purpose. You can use kundalini energy to enhance your sexuality or transform it so you can be celibate. You need to meditate on your purpose in your body and how you need to use these powerful creative energies.

Kundalini energy is the spiritual transformer. It can transform any physical energy into a higher vibration to be used for a spiritual purpose. Those who wish to

SEXUALITY AND KUNDALINI ENERGY

devote all of their energy to the service of God can translate their sexual and other body energies into a spiritual level that will give them the power to serve with a strong spiritual focus. Those who wish to create with more focus on the physical world can use kundalini energy to raise the vibration of the body to allow more of their energy into the physical realm. Kundalini energy can help you operate as spirit whether you wish to focus more into or out of the body. You are spirit, and you can learn to be in charge of your creations and energies, even the powerful creative force of sexuality.

BRINGING THE BODY
TO AN AWAKENED STATE

The human body is an alive, dynamic vehicle for the soul. We, as spirit, have invested a great deal of energy in the physical world and in our bodies. Many beings have lost their awareness of themselves as spirit because they have invested so much of their energy in the physical world of matter. Many have come to believe they are their bodies and that there is nothing but the physical world.

This sleeping state is what many people on Earth are now experiencing. The lack of awareness of the spiritual nature of all things and the spirituality of humanity is the main cause of disturbance on this planet. The lack of spiritual information is perpetuating this state of unawareness. While many people seek God, they seek God outside of themselves instead of within. This outward focus for spiritual information and guidance can cause confusion and create power games and control games instead of the spiritual awakening of the individual soul.

For the soul to reawaken to its spiritual nature, it must realize that it is not its body and does not have the characteristics of the body. The body operates in time and space, is limited by effort, competition and ethics, and is mortal. The spirit operates outside of time and space, does not have competition, ethics or effort, and is immortal, to list a few of the differences. The soul needs to learn to have affinity for its body to create fully through it since the affinity for the body's characteristics helps the soul work through the medium of the body.

The differences between spirit and body cause a great deal of confusion for many people seeking spiritual information and awakening. The person may start her spiritual opening with good intentions and end up focused on an ego trip, in pain, or in fear because she did not know the difference between spirit and body. Trying to make the body like the spirit is impossible, and trying to make the spirit like the body is also impossible. Unfortunately, many people get caught in exactly that pattern. This attempt to make one like the other disrupts the natural affinity between a spirit and its body. It can make the body afraid of spirit and cause spirit to spend its energy outside of the body.

To bring the body back to an awakened state, it is essential to recognize the differences between spirit and body and not try to make the body be like you, the spirit. A spiritually awake body is very different from a spiritually awake soul. The body's natural characteristics

are intensified when the body is healed. Thus, the
sexuality, emotionality, and other physical characteristics
are stronger and require more spiritual attention to turn
them to spiritual use. The differences between spirit and
body are the same whether the soul or body is asleep or
awake. The body is still mortal and the soul is still
immortal. The body uses effort, time and space, and
spirit does not. An awakened body is one through which
the spiritual energy flows easily, and healing is constantly
occurring as the spirit takes responsibility for its
intensified energy field. If spirit wakens its body and does
not care for it, the body can be a powerful vehicle that is
out of control.

Bringing the body to an awakened state requires
healing it by clearing the lies, foreign energy,
misinformation, past-time energy, and other
inappropriate energies from it. It means clearing
anything from your body that is not in agreement with
your spiritual nature such as hate, fear, pain, and the ego
that covers all of your mistakes. An awakened body is an
alive body, unencumbered by the energies which deaden
it, such as pain and the other energies already mentioned.
Once a body begins to awaken, the healing focus must be
increased so the disturbances stored in the body do not
get you off your spiritual path. An awakened body is an
exciting challenge to use. It is like riding a healthy,
spirited horse instead of a sick, jaded one.

Kundalini energy is a wonderful healing vibration for

spiritualizing the energy you have invested in these inappropriate energies in your body. You can take energy you have stored in past pain experiences and transform it to a neutral energy which you can reuse in the present in a more beneficial manner. You can transform any energy you do not like or want into present-time neutral energy for your spiritual creativity. You can also use kundalini energy to spiritualize the new vitality of your body. You can use kundalini to help you use your new sexual or emotional vitality for a spiritual purpose. You are meant to be fully awake and alive, spiritually and physically, as you are a child of God.

Unfortunately, we often waste our energy and talents. One of my students had a great deal of her energy invested in her anger with her mother. She had meditated for several months to clear this fury but was making slow progress. When she discovered her kundalini energy, she was delighted. She said that she was able to move the anger very fast and regain her spiritual perspective about her mother. She saw that the kundalini energy transformed her fury rapidly, without effort. This helped her avoid judging herself for her emotions toward her mother, which had stopped her healing process. The fast cleansing of her anger helped her move to a neutral perspective where she could experience her affinity for her mother.

Kundalini energy raises our vibration to a spiritual level where we can overcome judgment, competition, effort, intellectualizing, and all of the other ways the body operates. The student's usual meditation did not move her energy above her body's emotional control, so she was caught in her old pattern. Kundalini energy moved her above the physical levels to the spiritual perspective, and she changed and healed. By using kundalini energy in her meditations, the student has started the process of awakening herself and her body. She is more alive and vital now than she was as a child. She is also using the kundalini energy to help her gain control of the awakened emotions of her body.

Kundalini energy is the best way I know to spiritualize the body and bring it to the level of vitality we need to accomplish our spiritual goals. I was having difficulty writing and could not gain my spiritual perspective about what was blocking my creativity. I meditated and did some necessary healing work and still did not regain joy in my work. I turned up my kundalini energy and was quiet. It did not take a great deal of time to move the disruptive energy when I let go of effort and allowed the kundalini energy to move through me and spiritualize my system. As usual, I was busy trying to solve someone else's problems instead of minding my own business. Since I do not like to see this weakness in myself, I allowed my intellect to get in the way as I sought an answer that I would like. This put me in effort because I did not want to look at the truth, and I had to use energy to avoid seeing it. The kundalini energy simply transformed the desire to perfectly heal and the belief that I could be responsible for anyone else, to neutral energy which I could use to write. The vibration of the kundalini energy was high enough to avoid my intellect saying, "It couldn't be that responsibility-for-others pattern again. It must be something else!"

Kundalini helps us operate as spirit and move above the body's patterns. It helps us cleanse the body and transform old patterns and unwanted energies to useful neutral energy we can use for our spiritual creativity. Just as I stopped my creative flow with an old pattern by putting my attention on trying to solve someone else's problem, we all get sidetracked and need to rise above the body patterns to change them. The use of kundalini energy continues to cleanse the body throughout life to develop and maintain a clear spiritual field in the body.

You need to respect the way the body operates to bring it back to an aware state. The body operates in time and through space, and you have to work with this aspect of physical reality to make things work in the body. It is necessary to validate that the body uses effort for everything it does and that it competes to survive. When you take these physical characteristics into consideration, you are able to work with them instead of resisting the body. You can even learn to have fun with your body as you create through it. Competition and effort can be fun if they relate to physical reality and you know what you are doing.

You can best accomplish what you are here to do by accepting and validating the reality into which you are creating. You can bring your spiritual vitality into the physical world by acknowledging how it works and working with and through the physical characteristics. You will sabotage yourself if you try to make your body operate like you as spirit. Your body will rebel if you suddenly stop sleeping, eating, having sex, and doing the other survival-oriented things the body needs. Your body will rebel if you do not allow it the time and space it needs to make changes in order to operate on a more spiritual level. It can take several lifetimes to accomplish some levels of seniority with bodies. You may spiritualize different aspects in several bodies before you achieve the level of spiritual seniority you seek. You do not have to give up the body's characteristics to be senior to the body.

Your body will not be happy or cooperative if you do not have affinity for it and take responsibility for it. Many years ago, a woman who was completing an intensive spiritual training program gave me a gift to thank me for the help I had given her during her training. She asked if there was anything she could do for me. I immediately said, "Learn to love yourself." She stepped back from me in shock and responded, "That is too much to ask." I have not seen this woman for over fifteen years. Even though she had accomplished the challenge of recognizing her spirituality and spiritual abilities, she ran away from the challenge of learning to love herself. Loving one's self is a much more challenging task than most people acknowledge as it requires that we take responsibility for our body and our creations and accept ourselves as we are. We have to validate both body and spirit to be awake on either level.

If you do not validate your body, it will push you out and take control to create what it wants as it will believe that you are the enemy and are trying to kill it. You may then find your physical creations focused totally on body-oriented desires such as food, housing, clothing, sex, and other survival issues. This can be fun for a short time but may not allow you to accomplish your spiritual goals. You need to validate that you are spirit with spiritual characteristics and you are creating through your body which has physical characteristics. You can think of it as similar to riding a horse. You have to know that you and the horse are different and that you are supposed to be in charge of where you are going.

A woman I have known most of my life does not acknowledge her spirituality. I have lamented over the fact that I cannot solve her problems or help her see that she is spirit and a part of God. I hope to spiritually mature to the level that I can accept her physical focus and stop trying to change her. When I accept that she does not want to relate to God, she will probably disappear from my life as I will no longer need her as a teacher. She is definitely with me to help me give up trying to take responsibility for others and allow everyone to be where he or she is as well as to highlight for me where I am physically focused.

This woman has tried every physical thing I can think of to make herself happy. She created social popularity, physical wealth, travel adventures, cosmetic surgery, diets, exercise programs, sexual affairs, and everything else advertised to find happiness. She admitted to me that she thought money would make her happy, but it did not. I have sent her books, talked to her, given her spiritual readings and healings and cannot reach her. This woman is an excellent example of someone who does not want to see the differences between spirit and body, so her body is in charge of everything she creates. Even though she is wealthy, she is so survival-oriented that her attention is always on housing, clothing, physical appearance, sex, or some other survival issue.

This woman's survival orientation keeps her, as spirit, out of her body and causes her body to be afraid. Her body is so afraid that she spends most of her time trying to control everything around her instead of getting to know herself, her body, and her other creations. Her body is not healthy, her family is constantly disturbed by her control games, and she is as far away from the happiness she seeks as a person can get in spite of the physical bonanza she has created. She is an excellent example that physical things cannot make a person happy.

Life is empty and meaningless without God and an

awareness of yourself as spirit. My friend could have everything she ever wanted if she would wake up to her spirituality and her connection with God. Like many people, she is lost in the darkness of spiritual sleep, and her body and the disturbances she has stored in it are in charge of her creativity. Unfortunately, this causes the body to sicken since spirit is what gives the body life.

Spirit is the light and life of the body. Without spirit, the body is like a survival machine, even if it is in the midst of plenty. The body can have more vitality and energy than anyone realizes if the spirit is in charge. The people who work closely with me often ask me how I manage to accomplish so much physically and also have time to meditate and be quiet. I tell them that I am operating the body as spirit, instead of letting the body be in charge, and that I take very good care of my body because it works hard for me. I acknowledge the differences of spirit and body and thus gain the optimum results of operating in both realms. I am still learning and gaining experience, and each new awakening reassures me of the importance of owning and loving my body.

You can experience an awakened body and an aware spiritual state in your body. You can most easily do this through meditation as a way to turn within to your spiritual self. You can attain a new level of affinity for your body when you accept yourself as spirit and accept your body as it is. This affinity can bring you a new working relationship with your body and a new state of awareness as spirit.

Every soul is here on Earth to learn and to teach. Every soul with a body has spiritual goals and a purpose. The understanding and correct use of the body is part of the game we learn on Earth. Kundalini energy helps us spiritualize our body and other physical creations in order to accomplish our goals and fulfill our spiritual purpose. We are meant to be aware, vital and energetic, both physically and spiritually. We are part of God and when we function fully in this world, we come to life.

"Kundalini energy is a way back to an aware state, above the fear, pain, and death of the physical body."

HEALING PHYSICAL PROBLEMS

Kundalini energy is a wonderful healing energy. It is best known for its sensation of spiritual ecstasy, but is also a powerful healing vibration. It transforms the energy we have invested in physical creations into neutral spiritual energy which can be re-used for continued spiritual creation. Kundalini energy can change pain, emotions, sexuality, or other physical energies into a higher spiritual energy. Any physical problem can be transformed to a spiritual level. This does not always manifest in a manner that pleases the body.

Kundalini energy is a vibration with which miracles are created. The miracles are not always as people expect them to be, but kundalini creates spectacular change regardless of one's expectations. One student expected to use his kundalini energy to become famous and possibly rich as well. When he started using his kundalini energy consciously and regularly, he encountered a great deal of pain stored in his body. The kundalini energy stimulated the pain and the accompanying fear in his body as it started raising the vibration in his body. He did not acknowledge that the kundalini was clearing and healing old patterns, and he resisted the healing. Instead of letting go of the pain and fear, he started to create through his past painful patterns and did some things that were not acceptable to his social group. His use of kundalini energy did make him famous in his group as he was fired from his job because of his behavior. He became famous, but not in the way he expected. He started the kundalini healing process but did not complete it. He stopped and got caught in pain and fear since he would not acknowledge what he had created and what he needed to heal to fully use his body.

We are in a body to learn about spiritual creativity. We learn to create matter from pure energy. We learn how to manipulate energy within the limits we have established in matter. We learn how to change energy from one vibration and form to another. We learn to be creators within our personal universe. Kundalini energy is a major part of the creative learning process. Learning to recognize and consciously use kundalini energy is one of the main things we, as spirit, need to do if we wish to become spiritually senior in this physical world. Moving through the challenges is as important as experiencing the joys created by using kundalini energy.

Kundalini energy helps us transform energy from one form to another. If we have energy in the emotional form of fear, we can use kundalini energy to transform that fear to a neutral energy to be used for creativity. Kundalini energy creates and destroys and re-creates in a powerful way. We, as spirit, need to remember how to deal with this force of power to fully manifest our spiritual creativity in the physical world. Many people are afraid of the destructive aspect of kundalini energy, but that is part of the process. For transformation to occur, one form must be destroyed so another form can be created. The energy is not destroyed, but the form is.

An excellent example of something similar to kundalini energy is a volcano. The volcano is dormant and everything appears quiet and unchanging. Then the heat and gases rise through the Earth and explode out the top of the mountain destroying anything in the volcano's path. Depending on the type of volcano, the rock, dirt, and gas may explode in one giant burst destroying everything for miles around like Mt. St. Helens in Washington State. Or the volcano may emerge as a fountain of fire and the lava may flow underground burning everything in its path to the sea like the volcano Kilauea in Hawaii. The volcano changes a landscape into an entirely new reality. It moves a mountain to the sea, pours soil in new areas, destroys and creates at the same time. No one sees the destruction of the volcano as being bad, except possibly someone whose property is destroyed.

The kundalini energy can rise relatively gently and flow smoothly like Kilauea or violently like Mt. St. Helens depending on the individual's growth process. I recommend the slow, gentle method of turning on kundalini energy since the energy is so powerful. Kundalini energy does not need extra force to be dramatic any more than a volcano does. Use the power of kundalini gently, and the landscape of your life can be transformed without so much drama or trauma. You do not need to judge your kundalini experience any more than you would judge a volcano. Both are forces of transformation. You can learn to control your kundalini experiences and use them to heal yourself.

Like the changes caused by a volcano, with the earth being distributed to new areas hundreds of miles away, kundalini energy moving through your body can change your reality drastically. Most people have created pain in their body in the process of being born, growing up, and living life. This old pain is stored in the body as memory, both conscious and subconscious. We, as spirit, create through memories of pain believing these to be the only reality available to us. Like the people living near the volcano, we believe our landscape is forever. We can change our physical system as much as a volcano changes the landscape, by using our kundalini energy to transform the pain energy to neutral energy, to be reused in a new creative form. This healing can release us from living with and creating through pain.

Meditation is necessary to achieve the awareness you need to use kundalini energy to heal yourself. You can achieve a level of awareness to harness your kundalini through meditation. You can then transform the energy you have invested in pain or fear or ego into energy to use for new creations. It can be as easy as changing your money from one investment plan to another. You can change any form of energy you have created to another form by using your kundalini energy.

There can be great joy in transforming your system from a heavy, physically-oriented one to a light spiritually-oriented system. Life can take on new meaning when you change your perspective of life by transforming your old concepts into new beliefs that relate to your spirituality and your present reality. You may be operating your life from beliefs that you adopted from your grandmother, and they do not work in your present circumstances. Your energy is tied up in these beliefs and not available for you to use to create what you want. Kundalini energy spiritualizes these ideas to be reformed into ones that work in the present. You can use kundalini to destroy old concepts and create new concepts.

If you believe that you have to be a victim to circumstances as your grandmother taught you, then you will create as a victim. If you are a corporate executive, this can cause a great deal of conflict in your life. You may be in charge at work, since your grandmother did not have ideas about that, but a victim at home. This dichotomy in your life could create confusion and even trauma. You can use kundalini energy to transform your adopted beliefs to a neutral energy to be used in the way you want to in the present.

We create everything in our lives to help us learn and grow. We create our family members, and then learn about the world from them. We create problems to help us learn. We create problems to solve, and thus grow wiser about ourselves and the world. We can learn to solve our problems from a spiritual perspective, and thus gain a great deal more in the process than if we view the problem from strictly a physical point of view. Kundalini energy can help transform our view of a problem from the physical to the spiritual. We can learn to see a problem as a learning opportunity.

The change of perspective alone can be a healing. When a friend of mine was diagnosed with cancer many years ago, she was at first very afraid. After meditating and working on gaining her spiritual perspective, she started to see the cancer as an important healing opportunity. Once she had the view of this creation as a possible healing, that is exactly what she made of it. She used her kundalini energy to help her clear past painful experiences from her body, once she had the realization that the cancer was caused by these old experiences stored in her system. My friend cured her cancer because she transformed her energy from pain, fear, and hate to hope and love. She is an inspiration to everyone she knows and has a powerful healing effect on others. Most people do not know what a transformation she created in herself. They do know she is a healing presence.

I have witnessed numerous healing miracles. Many of the healings manifested rapidly because of the use of kundalini energy. These fast healings or miracles have varied from a headache disappearing in seconds to a lump in someone's chest disappearing in a few weeks. People are natural healers and often simply need information to help them focus correctly to solve their problem. Kundalini energy can help you with any healing project, whether physical or spiritual.

We create problems and we make mistakes to learn things. If we do everything perfectly, we are not learning. Most successful artists, writers, business people, athletes, ministers, construction workers, and so forth have many failures and mistakes before they gain success. A child learning to walk falls down. A young person learning to read stumbles with words before he learns to read them. Whatever we do, we make mistakes as we learn. The mistakes allow us to grow and do better. In fact, our mistakes often teach us more than our successes. Whatever mistake we have made, we can transform into success by making it a lesson instead of a failure.

We can use kundalini energy to transform the energy tied up in guilt or remorse over our mistakes and create neutral energy to help us continue to create. We can learn to enjoy our mistakes on our way to gaining our goals. The kundalini energy gives us back the energy we invest in the mistake, such as anger, guilt, or judgment and allows us to move on to create what we want. It transforms us from a static state to a state of motion. It moves us above the emotions and judgment often associated with mistakes and allows us to enjoy all of our creations.

Kundalini energy is a powerful vibration. It can help us transform our problems and debilitating patterns into neutral energy for our continuing creative work. All it takes to begin the transformation is a willingness to operate as spirit. During a recent personal healing project, I was clearing old emotional pain and the fear the body experienced from past experiences. I became so involved in the clearing process that I got lost in the past experiences and felt a great deal of fear for several hours. I soon remembered that I am spirit and not my body. I used my kundalini energy to move out the fear and past experiences. The kundalini energy transformed the past memories into neutral energy and helped me move my attention back into the present where my body resides. In a short time, I was involved in a new creative project and my body was happy instead of afraid.

Kundalini energy heals the physical body by cleansing inappropriate energies such as pain, fear, and hate. These energies must first come up before they come out. Many people get caught in fear when the body begins to heal, and they stop the healing process. Commitment to spiritual healing is needed to use kundalini energy fully since you need to move through whatever you have started. Once you begin using kundalini energy for your healing, it is important to keep going until you finish the process.

Your body will also experience a desire to be healthy as you clear the unhealthy energy with kundalini. It may want more water, exercise, better food, rest, or whatever it needs. A friend of mine was shocked when she asked her body what it wanted to eat and it responded, "Salad." She often ate fast foods and thought her body liked this, but it was actually a convenience for her, as spirit, so she could work her body more. She is slowly learning to respond to her healthier body with new patterns.

Kundalini energy is useful in everyday life as well as in meditation as it can move you from fear or depression to peace or joy. It can replace external methods of changing your moods and put your power back into your own control. Kundalini energy can help you create a healthier, happier body. Kundalini energy is a spiritual blessing, and you can relearn how to use it to take control of your body and your creativity.

Pain, Fear, Death and Other Body Games

As spirit, there is no pain, fear, or death. We have these and other physical experiences only when we are in a physical body. The spirit usually begins to experience pain and fear in the fetal state since the fetus experiences the same reality as the mother, and most adults create an abundance of fear and pain. If the fetus experiences a great deal of pain and fear, it will be born with the belief that this is what life is like on planet Earth. A friend whose mother was beaten during her pregnancy with him never recuperated from the pain, fear, and resulting hate he stored in his body from this early abuse. He accomplished a great deal during his life, but his body contained such deep-seated patterns of pain and fear that he never became completely free of these patterns, even though he used kundalini.

Life in a body is intended to be a learning game. If we forget that life is a game, we can easily get lost in a state of seriousness, heaviness, emotionality, pain, or apathy. Spirit is light, powerful, joyous, and a part of God. Spirit does not have to lose all of these characteristics when it enters a body. Spirit can retain its sense of fun and play as it learns and grows while creating through matter. We, as a spiritual group called human beings, have lost much of our spiritual awareness, and therefore our sense of life as a game. We are caught in many of the physical patterns we have created and now believe these patterns are reality. We created the games and got lost in them. We can change the games. We do not have to be lost in fear, pain, death, or the other physical games we have created, regardless of their intensity or origin. We can transform our energy to a spiritually awakened state of awareness and see our life in bodies as a creative, learning, growing game. We can deal with pain, fear, and death from a spiritual level where we can experience our creative power.

Creating on Earth can be an adventure, from conception to death. But for many people, the beginning, with the process of conception and birth, is a painful experience, so they begin their physical life in pain and fear. We need to take responsibility for our sexuality to provide high energy healing levels for conception and birth. Unfortunately, in Western society, conception and birth are not recognized as important spiritual experiences and the birth process has been interfered with to such an extent that it is more painful than necessary. Women who are spiritually aware often have spiritual experiences and little pain during the birth; this makes it a more pleasant experience for the mother and the baby. Pain and trauma at birth can become detrimental to the soul's creativity unless acknowledged and cleared. Many of the problems people go to psychiatrists to solve relate to their birth experience. Since the memory of their birth has been with them during their entire life, they believe that the pain is their present reality. If someone is not spiritually aware, it can take hypnosis for the person to recognize his or her problem as a birth trauma. Meditation can lead one to remember these early experiences without the assistance of another person. Kundalini meditation can help heal these painful experiences.

One woman who had meditated for several years had a healing opportunity when she gave birth to her daughter, but she was unwilling to face her past experiences. The woman's own birth was Caesarean. She had worked through some of the disturbance she had during her birth experience, but had not dealt with her fears about her ability to have a natural birth. When her daughter was born, she was unable to overcome her fears, gained during her own birth, and her daughter was also born by Caesarean. The daughter, who is now seven years old, recently said that she did not believe that she would be able to have children since she could not give birth. She adopted her mother's belief system, without even discussing it. Fortunately, an adult friend helped the child understand that she could create whatever she wanted.

Another story concerns a woman who was about to

give birth. She started to experience debilitating fear about the birth process. She came to me for a spiritual reading, and I saw that she was dealing with someone else's birthing experience and a fear of dying from childbirth. She confirmed this as she remembered that when she was a child, her aunt had died during childbirth, and she had experienced everyone's fear about this. She cleared the childhood fears about her aunt's experience and created a joyous birth for herself and her daughter.

The human species has gotten in the habit of creating pain and fear from the beginning of its material existence. We have become so accustomed to these vibrations that we believe they are more important than they are and that we cannot do without them. We have forgotten that pain and fear are the experiences of the body and not of the soul. Pain and fear are even overrated on a body level as they are simply survival techniques. These survival methods have grown in importance in human society to the point that there are entire industries built around them. We have enormous drug, medical, and psychiatric industries focused on pain and fear. These industries are making vast sums of money, but they do not appear to be having the desired success of helping people with their deeper problems.

A major problem is the focus on the body and the survival aspect of the body, without consideration for the spiritual aspect of creation. If the spiritual aspect of conception, pregnancy, birth, life, and death were considered, we would begin with much less pain and fear and have an easier time clearing the pain and fear we have created. Our kundalini energy would be a natural part of creativity, and we would not be caught in the endless round of physical games. We would not create as much pain, and thus would not have as much pain to clear from the body. We would know that we are spirit and not the body.

Once a soul has experienced pain in the womb and at birth, it is in a body containing pain, and thus the soul is operating through pain in all of its physical creations. This is not the hopeless state many would have you believe it to be. You can clear these past pain experiences with meditation and with kundalini energy, and then be clear to create in a state of spiritual freedom. Pain is an energy and can be changed and healed. A spirit can learn to transform the pain or to transform its relationship with the body and move above the pain. Either way, the spirit is no longer controlled by pain in its creative process.

We are usually so focused on the body and its survival that we create the opposite of what we want in many situations. Instead of creating a peaceful loving pregnancy and joyous birth experience, we often create pain and fear. The little body which is surrounded with disturbance, at these times, lives a disturbed life unless she meditates and clears these experiences. In adulthood, the body still contains the memories of the past pain and fear and operates on these signals. The soul, creating through the body, sees the world through the painful experiences and creates according to their messages.

Since pain and fear are part of the body's survival system and we have emphasized these vibrations to the point of obsession, we have created societies based on these survival games. Some religious groups have even gotten into the game of manipulating people through fear and pain. The thing we have forgotten is that we are spirit and we create our life on Earth. We have created the fear and pain, and we can change it. If we have pain from childhood and fearful memories from the past, we can learn to meditate to deal with them. Through meditation, we can learn the purpose of the experiences and use kundalini energy to transform the pain into neutral energy to be used in a different manner.

Throughout life, we continue to create pain and fear in the body. We create childhood injuries in our attempt to satisfy the expectations of the adults around us and to satisfy our curiosity and growing egos. We look around us and match the people we admire and fear, and create many of the mistakes they have created. We then learn that it is not socially acceptable to show pain or fear, so we create a wall of lies to pretend that we are fine and do not have pain or fear. This wall of protection is our ego and often the most difficult part of our energy system to change.

We play so many games based on the survival of the body that we get lost in the complexity of these games and lose the awareness of ourselves as spirit. This is one way we numb the body. We fill it with pain, fear, and other disturbance, and then surround it with a facade to pretend that we are fine and do not have pain or fear. We deaden the body so much it is difficult to use. This game is one that we can stop and even reverse. We can meditate and learn to know ourselves as spirit. We can use our spiritual energies to clear the inappropriate energies we have stored in the body and bring the body back to life.

Kundalini energy can be an important factor in this enlivening process. Whatever you have created or stored, you can use kundalini energy to transform it into spiritual energy to use in your conscious creative process. It is best to take time for these transformations to occur. The body operates in time, and you will be changing the body, so you need to consider the body's characteristics as you change. You change your system a great deal by transforming one image of pain into neutral energy. Allow time for your body to adjust to the healing, and you will create in harmony with your body.

Many people who meditate eventually turn on their kundalini energy without consciously focusing on it. A woman called me because she had difficulty with her kundalini energy and an acquaintance had referred her to me. She was so afraid of her kundalini energy that her fear was controlling her experience. She had clearly received misinformation about kundalini energy. She believed that it was totally dangerous and that she could not control it. I reassured her that she could learn to be in control of her kundalini energy and enjoy it a great deal. I suggested she go to our center in Portland, Oregon, to get a healing and more information, since she lived near there. I later learned that she had been taught how to consciously turn her kundalini energy on and off, but she did not wish to take responsibility for it or what it stimulated in her. Maybe she was like a virgin who does not want to be responsible for her "seduction." Ah, the sweet pain of irresponsibility.

You can learn to be responsible for your life and all you create, including your kundalini energy. You can learn to turn on your kundalini energy without waiting for it to turn on. More important, you can learn to turn it off when you wish, so you are in control of this powerful flow of energy. This way, you can clear a past pain experience, and then turn your kundalini energy down or off to let the body adjust before you use your kundalini energy to heal more. You can learn to be in touch with your body and work with it to create a joyous and healing kundalini experience, without being overwhelmed by your physical creations.

A man who had a very disturbed childhood and experienced a great deal of pain and fear throughout his youth discovered meditation and then kundalini energy in his late twenties. At the beginning of his healing process, he was so excited about kundalini energy that he overused it and disturbed his body. He did not want to hear anything about moderation, so his body began to fear him because he was forcing it to change at a rate it could not handle. He eventually heard that he had become his body's enemy instead of its friend, and he started communicating with his body. He saw how disturbed his body was and established a more moderate healing program. He learned to run his kundalini gently through his system, instead of like a freight train, and developed affinity for his body.

We are in the habit of misunderstanding and misusing our bodies so much that we often continue to misuse our bodies during our healing process. Kundalini energy can easily be misused. It can be run so strongly that it is a trauma to the body. The body will rebel and the healing will not occur. The kundalini energy can become destructive if misused or abused. It is important to learn to control kundalini energy so it has the healing effect we seek. It is also necessary to communicate with the body and to take responsibility for oneself to use kundalini energy safely. It takes time for the body to adjust to experiencing a great deal of kundalini energy, so we need to have patience with the process of creating through a body.

Death is another aspect of the body's reality that we do not have as spirit. The body dies, the spirit does not. Death is also a body characteristic with which we have become obsessed. We are no longer senior enough to the body to accept its death as a part of its existence. This indicates how much we have come to worship our bodies instead of ourselves as spirit and our God. The funeral industry is a large business because of people's worship of the body and subsequent fear of death. Some people believe in the preservation of the body because they believe it is the only one they will ever have. The business of freezing bodies has developed because people have spirit and body confused. In the future, people may want to clone themselves. What spirit will inhabit the clone? Do you want an unknown entity that looks exactly like you creating in the world? An awareness of reincarnation ends many of the body games about death, as one becomes aware of having occupied many bodies. Reincarnation validates a continuing learning process for spirit manifesting in many bodies. Reincarnation allows for a realistic, respectful relationship with the body, and for its death.

As spirit, we have had many bodies and will have many more. We decide everything about the body before taking it such as its parents, siblings, gender, genetic make up, lessons, and how it will die. We can change many of these things during life if we complete a cycle and are ready for a new lesson. We can change how we die if we change our beliefs. An unaware life may become a spiritually awakened one, and the death of the body could change from one of pain and fear to a spiritual transition of peace and calm.

Before written history, spirit would use the body until it had fulfilled its purpose for it and then lay the body down and leave it. There was no grief, fear, or pain involved in leaving a body. It was as simple as taking off old clothes. Today, we have invested so much energy in the body that we hold on to it beyond its usefulness. We allow the body to be in charge, and therefore it creates life around its survival instincts. We connect bodies to machines, operate on them, and keep them alive, at all cost. Our modern medical procedures are a beneficial part of our healing options, but for many, the bodies take charge of this aspect of spiritual creativity and the spiritual perspective is lost. Fewer and fewer societies and religions teach the truth about death than was so in the past. Many groups take advantage of people's ignorance and fears about the death of the body and perpetuate the focus on survival, instead of on God.

For spirit, birth and death are the same. They are a transition from one reality to another. Kundalini energy can help spirit regain its seniority with the body in relation to the body's death. The more a soul uses kundalini energy in the body to raise its vibration and cleanse the inappropriate energies, the more it gains seniority with the body. The body eventually becomes the vehicle for the soul instead of being the one in charge of the creative process in the physical world. Kundalini energy can then be used to help create a spiritually aware death for the body, controlled by spirit, without pain or fear.

I have had several near-death experiences. Some of them were more fun than others. One time, for a few seconds, I believed that I was dead and experienced a wonderful inner peace. When I realized the body was alive, the experience changed completely as the body survival instincts took control. This happened when I was in my early twenties. I was fishing on the rocky cliffs on the coast of California, north of the Golden Gate bridge in San Francisco. We took a break from fishing to climb down on the rocks to collect mussels for bait. As I was bending down to get a fine fat mussel, a large wave washed over me, taking me into the sea. There was a giant rock just offshore from where I was, and I hit my back against it, and then shot through the channel which ran between the cliffs and the rock. I left my body for a short time, and when I returned to my body, I had the thought that I was dead; I felt so peaceful. All I saw was blue and I felt weightless. This was, of course, the water around me. When I looked up, I saw that I was under water, and I could see the light of the sun. Survival was a possibility and was immediately number one on my list of priorities. I swam as fast as possible toward the light and the surface.

Since I, the spirit, was thrown out of my body without warning, the body believed it was dead. As spirit, I was happy to be free of the body. The body and the consciousness of the body were happy to discover I was alive. This dichotomy, of immortality and mortality, is part of learning to balance the dichotomy of being spirit in a body. At the time of this experience, I was not as spiritually awake as I am now; even then, I knew that I was much more than my body. As I processed and evaluated the experience, I remembered a great deal that I had forgotten from this life and past lives. The physical shock of the experience, plus the spiritual aspect of it, brought up information from my subconscious memory that helped me awaken spiritually. I do not recommend creating accidents or trauma of any kind to spiritually reawaken, although many people use this method. Meditation is much more pleasant and works better, with no damage to the system to heal later.

Most everyone is afraid of death because people often are not aware of themselves as spirit. People believe they are just the body, so the death of the body is frightening since it appears to be the end of all consciousness. Death of the body is not the end of consciousness. It is the beginning of a new consciousness. Just as birth puts the soul's awareness into the physical world, so death puts the soul's attention back into the spiritual realm. We can gain mastery over the experience of creating in matter, to the level of learning to take all of the information we gained in a life, into the next stage of development. Our information can become immortalized if we learn to ground from the first chakra and use our kundalini energy to transform our energy into spiritual levels for use after the body's death.

Death is a body phenomenon. Only the body dies. Spirit is immortal and never dies. We change form from one life to another and from one spiritual state to another. It is necessary to gain a spiritual perspective to see the immortality of spirit and the mortality of the body. It is necessary to be spiritually oriented and neutral to truly accept this spirit-body difference. We need to learn about energy and how to manipulate it to change forms and create what we want in order to be senior to death.

Kundalini energy is a powerful tool for us to use as spirit to transform our perspective from the physical to the spiritual. It transforms everything from the material to the spiritual. Kundalini energy helps free the soul from a focus on the body, the body's desires, and its other physical creations. A total focus on the body enslaves the spirit in the world of matter. There is a great deal of energy invested in the world of matter, and many groups are devoted to controlling souls to keep their attention and energy tied up in the material realm. These groups believe that the material world, with its physical power, is all there is, and program others to believe the same. Anyone who believes in the spiritual realm is a threat to them as the spiritual believer challenges their materialistic beliefs and power games. Political dictators are a good example since they usually try to destroy all religious and spiritual groups in order to maintain power over people.

There are groups actively involved in keeping souls

asleep and in their control. There are individuals who believe that controlling others is more important than worshipping God. These individuals and groups are not limited to one society or one aspect of society. The controllers can be found in governments, religions, schools, businesses, industries, military organizations, families, crime societies, and in every other area of society. Anyone who wants to control the creativity of another soul creating within its own personal space is attempting to limit or stop that soul's creativity and growth. Anyone attempting to control others is not spiritually focused.

These materialistic individuals and groups believe that matter is more important than spirit. They are attempting to create a sense of spiritual death. When the individual soul is not moving and creating, it feels heavy, apathetic, and like death. When the soul is awake and creating, it experiences its flow of life force energy and its creativity and communication. Many people are experiencing a living death since they are allowing someone or something outside of themselves to control them and their creative process. How many drugs, both legal and illegal, would lose popularity if people were spiritually awake? This one issue illustrates how much opposition there is to spiritual awakening since some people would lose a great deal of money without the popularity of drugs. How many aspects of society would change if people became spiritually aware and took control of their creativity?

Many social conventions have become like drugs because they cause the individual to turn their energy down and conform with the group to the extent that the individual's spark is controlled and dimmed. The soul then experiences a death-like state as spirit and believes that death is a state of both body and soul. Even in religion, we find organizations which have moved away from their original teachings and are involved in programming the group to conform to social conventions instead of worshipping God. The death-like states that are created by so many situations in modern society are disturbing to people and interfere with the intended spiritual creativity. Kundalini energy can help awaken people and bring them to a vital, creative state of being. People can re-learn to create as spirit.

The fear of death that has resulted from a lack of awareness of ourselves as spirit and a separation from God causes many of the problems we experience today. People stop creating and enjoying life when they are focused on the death of the body. They live in a state of fear. Their creativity slows, and may even stop. They may become closed in on themselves to the point that they no longer interact with others. The fear of death is a disease in modern society. There are many who take advantage of this spiritual illness by selling people things and ideas that are supposed to make them feel better, but instead deaden them more.

The fear of death exists because we have forgotten who we are and what we are here on Earth to do. We have filled our bodies with energies that do not belong in them and, as spirit, moved further away from our creative vehicle, the body. We move from an aware state at birth to an asleep state, usually by the age of three or four. Most people turn off their awareness because of social pressure to conform to the unaware state of the surrounding society. With the body filled with debilitating energies, we desert it, and our learning opportunity is lost until we either wake up or reincarnate into a new body and reality.

Kundalini energy is a way back to an aware state, above the fear, pain, and death of the physical body. The soul can wake up to its power and abilities and relearn to use spiritual energies to consciously create. Meditation is an essential part of waking up, and kundalini energy can be part of the cleansing process to transform the energy invested in matter back into spiritual energy. Meditation and kundalini energy are free, legal, and do not require the acceptance of anyone else's beliefs to use. Used correctly, they can help anyone return to a spiritually aware state.

We, as spirit, created our bodies as vehicles in the physical world, and then lost ourselves in our creation. It would be like creating a robot and forgetting that it is a mechanism we have made to do our bidding. We would then let the robot make all of our decisions and tell us what to do. The body is often the controlling factor in a soul's experience on Earth because the soul forgot itself while in the body. We need to consider the body and its characteristics, respect the body as our temple, and use it correctly, but we do not need to allow it to be in charge. If we allow the body to be senior to us as spirit, we are vulnerable to forces in the material world that want to control and use us; and there are many.

This immersion in the physical world is experienced by most everyone to some extent and can be reversed by meditating and using kundalini energy. This time on planet Earth is an opportunity for souls to wake up and remember who we are. We can wake up to the fact that we are spirit, a part of God, and the creators of our reality.

REGAINING A SPIRITUAL PERSPECTIVE

Here you are in a body, with many challenges and a desire to gain a spiritual perspective about your life. What do you do first? To begin, you need to desire a spiritual perspective. Second, you need to believe that you can achieve a spiritual perspective. If you persevere, you will gain your spiritual perspective. Meditation is the best way to develop your spiritual awareness and perspective. Your life is the playing field, and you are the creator of the game. You are the one who chooses what and how to play, hopefully respecting the other players as you create. It can be fun when you play your own game of life. Nothing is more interesting to you than your creative endeavors.

A spiritual perspective is a state of being and a way of relating to the body. Spirit has many abilities which are focused in the chakra system along the spine. Kundalini energy runs through channels in the spine and activates the chakras. The sixth chakra, which relates to spiritual sight, is where spirit needs to abide to have a clear spiritual perspective. Both the physical eyes and the spiritual "eye" are located in the head. This area is stimulated by kundalini energy and helps develop the ability to see clearly and neutrally as spirit.

Kundalini energy helps to activate and cleanse the sixth chakra so you can see spiritual reality, including vibrations, pictures, symbols, and formulas. You can learn to tell the truth from a lie and to see your spiritual path. To develop a spiritual perspective, you must commit to cleansing and clearing your personal space or you will continue to look through the veil of energy composed of concepts from the past, from others, and from lies that deflect you, the spirit. Cleansing and healing are a required part of using kundalini energy and developing a spiritual perspective.

In order to see life as spirit instead of as a body, it is helpful to realize that you and everyone you know have been taught a great many lies. Some of the lies that you have to let go of are: you are a body, you are mortal, you only have one life, you are a victim of circumstance, you must consider others first, it is better to give than to receive, and many more lies that deflect your spiritual perspective and create imbalance. There are very few absolutes in this world, and none of the preceding comments are absolutes, as you may believe. In many circumstances, it is better to receive so you do not invalidate the giver, or to take care of yourself first so you live to help others. I like the example of needing, during an emergency while flying, to put an oxygen mask on yourself first before you put one on your child. You need to be conscious to assist someone else. You are spirit and not your body, and you have had many lives and experienced many bodies. You are immortal spirit and the creator of your reality. If you do not know yourself, you are not prepared to relate to anyone else.

How many lies have you been taught about spirit? Can you count that high? Clearing the lies from your system helps you see life more clearly since lies cloud your view. Meditating on clearing the lies you have about yourself and others can help you begin to see everyone as spirit. It can help you see your creations as spiritual lessons. You see that you were given your physical space in which to create and need to stay in it instead of invading anyone else's space. You also see that no other soul has the right to create in your personal space. Spiritual perspective allows you to operate as spirit with respect for all living things and their space. Spiritual perspective can eliminate crimes of invasion. Life takes on new meaning and becomes more fun when you start seeing things as spirit instead of as a body through a veil of lies. You learn to respect yourself and others as creative spirit and to see God in all things when you clear your system.

Many lies have been taught about kundalini energy. These lies keep people from using this energy to establish or increase their spiritual perspective. Some of the lies that are taught are: kundalini energy cures all ills, it makes you celibate, it makes you spiritually evolved, it makes you crazy, it is dangerous, it makes you enlightened, and many other lies about this valuable vibration. Kundalini energy, without faith, will not cure anything. Kundalini energy does not make you celibate, but it can help you be celibate if you choose to be. Kundalini energy does not make a soul spiritually evolved. Many musicians and artists use kundalini energy to create their music and art, and they are not what some would call spiritually evolved. You may appear "crazy" to your society any time you operate from a spiritual level as you may not be fitting into the norm. Kundalini energy simply stimulates what is, and it is your responsibility to control your system. The misuse of any energy can be dangerous, whether it is spiritual or physical. People do not stop using dynamite because it is dangerous; they learn to use it correctly. Kundalini is simply an energy that you, as spirit, can learn to use for your creative expression.

To have a spiritual perspective of kundalini energy, you need to clear the lies about kundalini energy. It is like being programmed about a person. Your friend may tell you what a terrible person someone is, and when you meet him or her, you operate through this information. It may take you some time to clear your friend's opinion so you can see this other person clearly and make your own decision. This is true of kundalini energy. If you have read a great deal about kundalini from someone else's perspective, you may first have to get rid of that person's ideas about this energy. Whether the person had a wonderful or a horrible experience, you have to realize it was someone else's experience, and not yours. It would be like a pregnant woman believing her birthing process would be like another woman's when no two experiences are the same.

Experiencing kundalini energy is unique for every individual. Every kundalini experience is unique. Do not expect any of your kundalini experiences to be repeated since each kundalini experience is dealing with different circumstances and energies. Your expectations can become another lie about kundalini that will interfere with your use of the energy. Kundalini is an energy to be used by spirit. It is not a cure-all or magic potion. It is a neutral energy to learn how to use to bring your system back to a spiritually aware state.

You, as spirit, are meant to be in charge of everything in your system, including your kundalini energy. This energy does not control you, unless you allow it. Your body does not control you, unless you allow it to control you. Your spouse, children, parents, or anyone else does not control you, unless you allow them to take charge of your system. You are the spiritual creator of your physical circumstances. Unless you have relinquished control of your reality, you are in charge. God has given you all that you have, and it is up to you what you do with it.

Kundalini energy can be a part of your creative process. You, as spirit, are in charge of everything including your kundalini energy. There are many control games on this planet about kundalini that interfere with people learning about and using this powerful energy. These control games teach people many lies such as: only special people use kundalini energy; only spiritual teachers, monks, or priests use kundalini energy; kundalini energy has to be taught to you by an expert; kundalini energy is sacred; kundalini energy is dangerous for "ordinary" people to use. These lies are often an attempt to keep this powerful energy in the control of a few. Some people who use kundalini energy believe the lies and perpetuate them for their own reasons.

Most souls with a body can run kundalini energy. You do not have to be or become a spiritual teacher, monk, priest, or any other kind of specialist to use kundalini energy effectively in your life. You do not need a teacher of kundalini, although this can help you. Once you consciously turn it on, you will probably say, "Oh, that's what that is," since you may have been experiencing kundalini energy most of your life. Kundalini is no more sacred than any other spiritual energy available to us. Kundalini energy is for all who are willing to develop it, even us ordinary people. If you are personally responsible and have a minimum of information about it, you can use kundalini energy safely and with ease.

Your spiritual perspective will return rapidly as you clear the lies you have adopted as truth. You will soon see yourself as spirit and kundalini energy as the powerful transformer you have available to heal yourself. As you use kundalini energy to take charge of your spiritual creativity in the physical world, you gain a sense of peace and power that is not possible without the use of this energy.

You are spirit and a part of God. Kundalini energy is a vibration available to help you transition into the world of matter, and then to transform the energy you have invested in matter back to your spiritual vibration, both while you use the body and when you leave it. It is like buying a house and putting your money, time, and energy into your house for years, and then selling the house and getting the energy invested back from a large sale price. You put your energy into that physical creation, use it, and then you take the energy out to be reused elsewhere. You, as spirit, do this every time you take a body. You invest your energy in the body and your creations through that body, and then hopefully you transform the energy to your spiritual vibration to take with you into the next life or stage of development. Kundalini energy helps you and your body with the process.

Kundalini energy is wonderful and can become a part of your creative process. Your spiritual perspective of this energy will give you seniority with it, and the use of kundalini energy will help you regain seniority with your body. You are spirit and a part of God. You are meant to be senior to all things including your kundalini energy. Remember this and life is fun.

KUNDALINI AND PLANET EARTH

Planet Earth is a spiritual creation. It is an alive body of energy. Like the human body, the planet is a vehicle for the expression of spiritual creativity. Earth is energy in motion and is constantly changing. It is easy to observe the creative nature of Earth by viewing volcanoes, rivers, wind, rain, floods, glaciers, and many other Earth phenomena at work changing the planet. Humans often experience the power of this living planet through Earth changes such as earthquakes and hurricanes, and they are always in awe of its power. The Earth is powerful energy in motion.

Earth was created to provide a material space for spirit to create, learn, and grow. Earth is a living energy force, like the human body. The Earth was created as the larger body for the spiritual growth process of the human species. Just as an individual soul has a physical body in which to create and learn, the human species has a large physical body for its collective consciousness. The same process which takes place in a human body also takes place in the body of Earth. Like a human body, the Earth had conception or the planting of the idea; birth, the manifestation into matter; infancy; childhood; and now puberty. Eventually the planet will make it to adulthood, old age, and death, but we are far from those steps, as we measure time.

The human bodies and the planet have evolved to a level where the souls can more fully function through them. Just as a human body takes time to mature for the soul to work through it, so the planet also has taken time to develop into a force through which we can fully create. The stage we are now entering, at the beginning of the millennium, is similar to puberty in the human body. It is a stage moving from childhood to adulthood. It is a volatile stage where there is a great deal of learning and experimentation. It is a stage where we believe we are much smarter than we are. This is a dynamic and dangerous time for the planet, just as puberty is for the individual. Fortunately, most people make it through puberty, and we certainly will as a species, even though it may require some difficult lessons.

The human bodies have progressed from a focus on survival to an awareness of spirit. The planet has also progressed from a physical focus to increased spiritual activity. The awareness of spirit is growing. Twenty years ago, meditation was a strange concept to the Western world. Today, meditation is seen on television and discussed in magazines and books. Angels were considered a strange, if not weird, idea a few years ago, and now there are television series about angels. People are becoming more aware, and the awakening will continue and become more dramatic.

Planet Earth, like the human body, is a material body; energy slowed to form matter. We are spirit and are using this physical form to learn about creativity. The planet has similarities to the human body such as operating in time and space, having mass, and having other specific physical characteristics. We are here to learn to work with the planet for our creative lessons. We are waking up in some areas such as environmental awareness, human rights, global awareness, and communications. However, the majority of the world and its human inhabitants are still operating in the dark about the spiritual aspect of our creativity. The planet is helping people wake up as it changes and heals.

The human bodies on Earth have been and are still being misused, and so is the planet. Earth has been misused to the point of abuse in many situations. Our ability to abuse is growing as our industrial and technological expertise grows. We are learning to use power; we often misuse it before we learn how to use it as a benefit. The misuse of atomic energy is an excellent example of our childish misuse of power before we understood what we had, much less what it could do. People were used as experiments, and thousands were annihilated with the atomic bomb before it was known what power had been discovered.

The Earth is filled with power, and part of our job is discovering this power and learning how to harness and use it. We also need to learn how to work wisely with the power we discover. We need to give up acting like greedy children who do not want to share with others or try to use what they find for their personal benefit instead of the good of humankind. It is time to wake up to the fact that we are spirit and are all connected, and that we need to operate from a larger perspective than we have used in the past. A bomb set off in one part of the world affects the entire planet, just as a volcano exploding in one place affects the entire planet.

We have not been kind to our individual bodies or to our collective body, the Earth. We have some cleansing to do on our larger body as well as on our individual bodies. Kundalini energy can help with both cleansing processes. We need this powerful energy since we have created heavy vibrations to cleanse such as fear, hate, pain, and jealousy. We need a high vibration to transform the heavy energy we have created in matter back into a higher level for our spiritual use.

This powerful kundalini energy is now emanating from our planet Earth. Kundalini is latent in every cell and has now awakened in the Earth. We need to become aware of kundalini energy and learn how to use it. The planet has increased its vibration as we have increased our vibration in these bodies. The process of creating in matter and then spiritualizing the matter is happening with our larger body planet Earth as well as with our individual human bodies. The process of spiritualizing the matter invested in Earth can appear dramatic to us since the Earth is large and her growth process is sometimes traumatic to human bodies. We become more comfortable with the power of the Earth when we see that we are spirit and the creators of the creative process.

Since kundalini energy is in the planet and rising through it, we can all take advantage of this increased vibration to help us spiritualize our bodies and creations. Every spirit in a body is feeling this increased energy in one way or another. Some are afraid of it as they are afraid of change or of death. Some are excited but concerned since they do not know what is happening to them. Others are happy to experience this energy rising as they have been waiting and preparing for this time of spiritual growth.

You can take advantage of this high energy. You can learn about kundalini energy and use it to cleanse your system and raise your personal body vibration. You will be more comfortable with the increase in energy on the planet when you can match it or move above it. You are spirit and one of the creators of what is now happening. Once you awaken to this, you can overcome any fear you have of this powerful energy and learn to use it for yourself and the world.

Our affinity for planet Earth can be greatly increased by our use of kundalini energy as we transform our perspective to the spiritual realm and learn to understand and control the physical reality more fully. The Earth is a beautiful, creative body for us to use and enjoy. When we operate as spirit, we wake up to who we are, what we are doing, and how to use the Earth to its fullest extent. We are here to learn to be a part of the Cosmic Family. We have to grow and take responsibility for our individual bodies and our collective body to become an adult member of the Cosmic Consciousness. Kundalini energy can help us do this.

Be still and listen to your body and the body of Earth. You will eventually be able to hear the music of the planet. You can change your perspective of the physical world by gaining your spiritual perspective through meditation. You can learn to see your place in the Cosmic Pattern. Everyone has a path and can discover and follow it. Your body and the Earth are the learning ground for you, as spirit.

A friend of mine resisted her path for many years. She tried several alternatives, including spiritual work. Finally, she became angry and gained her personal space enough to see that she was trying to please others instead of doing what she was here to do. She was afraid of alienating her friends and family, but she went forward anyway. She quit her job with her church and started a small wholesale bakery business. She believed that her path was to bake the best bread possible to nourish people. She has stayed true to her path and now has a retail bakery and wholesale bread business. She has had to be brave as she met challenges and overcame problems.

She has also been generous and supportive to others as she created, and these gifts are returning to her. Her commitment and love for her work brought her support from others that astounded her.

My friend stayed true to herself and her path on Earth. There are as many paths to follow as there are people on Earth. Whether you are meant to perform as a baker, banker, parent, minister, farmer, teacher, construction worker, doctor or whatever, you can develop a spiritual perspective of your work and how it affects Earth. You can learn to respect individual creativity and let go of judgment of any profession, group, or way of creating. You can use kundalini energy to raise your perspective of creativity to a spiritual level for yourself and the planet.

When you create through love instead of fear, you have a powerful healing effect no matter what your calling is. Kundalini energy intensifies whatever you do, think, or feel, so know yourself; then you can have the impact you desire. Kundalini energy can help you cleanse the fear so you can increase the flow of love through you. This may be your greatest gift to the planet.

SPIRITUALIZING OUR PHYSICAL CREATIONS

Kundalini energy is a powerful transforming energy. You need a foundation of spiritual techniques to prepare you and continue to assist you in your use of this spiritual power. Everyone can learn to use it if they are willing to invest the time and attention. Kundalini energy is a blessing unless you do not know how to control it and how to turn it off. I like to compare kundalini energy to having hot water in your house. Your hot water is wonderful to turn on and have, but it would be a problem if you did not know how to turn it down and off. With your hot water running full blast all of the time, you would be hot, sweaty, and wet all of the time. You would develop rashes and skin problems. You could even develop back problems from bending down under the sink to figure out how to turn off the hot water.

This is a silly comparison, but hopefully it makes the point. If you do not know how to use something, whatever it is, you will have problems. Kundalini energy is powerful, so you need to learn to use it in order to avoid being overwhelmed by it. It is important to learn to turn it on slowly and gently so you stay in control. Just as the driver in a car needs to be in control to be safe, you need to be in control of your energy at all times. I cannot emphasize enough the careful use of spiritual techniques when turning on kundalini energy. I require students to complete sixteen weeks of courses in meditation and healing techniques before they can take the eight week kundalini class. The foundation in grounding and other spiritual techniques is invaluable.

You can benefit greatly from learning and using spiritual techniques to help you discover your spiritual nature and abilities. You develop your spiritual focus when you use spiritual techniques, just as you learn tennis by putting your attention on tennis techniques. It is easy to refocus as spirit if you use spiritual techniques to help you. If you seek to have a spiritually focused life, you must have spiritual tools to lay a firm foundation. Kundalini energy frees you from limits, uncovers your unique nature, and helps you realize your capabilities. Your spiritual tools keep you safely grounded in this Earthly reality, as you experience all of this.

Your body needs time to unlearn and learn. It has to unlearn the old patterns and limits, and it needs time to learn and adjust to the new patterns you create. If you have operated with the concept that you are a body for all of your life, it will take time to adjust to the fact that you are spirit and not your body. You will need time for your body to adjust to the changes you create by using kundalini energy and transforming your energy from a physical to a spiritual focus. You need to adjust to your new power and capabilities and how you want to use them. You need time to adjust to your true nature as you release your facades.

When you use kundalini energy, you are changing the energy in the body so you need to be aware of the body. Spiritual techniques can help you communicate with your body. They will also help you learn how to work with your body. You have to practice anything you teach the body so it can create a pattern to follow. Using spiritual techniques takes practice so you and your body can learn to operate together, as spirit in the physical world.

The Western world does not usually give permission for a spiritual focus unless you have chosen a spiritual vocation. Some Eastern societies allow for a spiritual focus regardless of profession, especially in later life. In India, it is not unusual for men to choose to leave their family and adopt a spiritual life in their later years. Regardless of your location or societal permission or lack of, you need to focus on your spirituality to awaken spiritually. Meditation is the best avenue to spiritual awakening, no matter where you live or what profession you follow.

The spiritual techniques presented here to help you meditate and awaken are: grounding, being centered in your head, creating and letting go of energy, running earth and cosmic energies, and turning kundalini energy on and off and running it. These techniques can help you spiritualize your physical creations. You can learn to turn impatience into patience, fear into love, pain into neutral energy, and hate into compassion. You, as spirit, can do anything you choose. You must practice and use the techniques for them to work for you. You cannot read about the techniques, intellectualize them, and then expect an effect. You must sit down and practice the techniques. You need to learn to ground before you turn on your kundalini energy; so practice it, and you will learn to be in control of your energy before you increase it.

It is important to remember to move through whatever you encounter in your system. If you discover hate, then face it and keep moving. Eventually, you will transform the hate into an energy you like. I know a woman who had the opportunity to transform her life from pain and fear to spiritual freedom. She was offered all manner of spiritual techniques and a great deal of help to learn and practice them. Early in her spiritual development, she encountered pain relating to being abused as a child. This is not uncommon and most people work through the issues. She refused to deal with these issues and used her new powers to cover up what she had found and to add new energy to her existing facades.

She was not as afraid of what had happened to her as she was afraid of what she had done to others later in her life. Since she had been abused and had not dealt with it in any way, she acted out her experiences with her children and abused her children. The abuse of her children is what she refused to face, so she could not deal with her own abuse issues as they would lead her to what she had done with her children. She did not move through what she found, so she is suffering even more than before her introduction to spiritual information because she has added energy to her existing pain and disturbance instead of facing and clearing it.

Whatever you find, you need to deal with and move through it, regardless of how horrible it may appear to you. If you do not, you make it worse by using spiritual techniques, especially kundalini energy, as you add great power to the energy you do not want. This woman is continuing to abuse her adult children as she is lying to them and programming them that nothing happened and everything is fine. Some of her children have found their own way to a spiritual perspective. Others are lost in a sea of pain, going to psychiatrists and taking drugs, in their attempt to deal with pain they do not understand. This woman could give her children a great gift by healing herself and spiritualizing her past pain. Instead, she chooses to invest more of her energy and attempts to invest her children's energy in protecting the pain of the past.

Spiritual techniques do not automatically guarantee blessings. It depends on how you use the spiritual techniques as to what effect they have on you and those around you. Kundalini energy does not guarantee any particular result. The results of your use of kundalini are dependent on your intent or desire and your faith or belief. It is completely up to you what you create. The use of spiritual techniques, including running kundalini energy, helps you gain a spiritual perspective and regain your spiritual abilities and energy. You can also use this power to add more energy to your existing physical reality such as your ego, facades, pain, and emotions. You can use the power to manipulate others, if you wish to create outside of your space. Spiritual techniques do not guarantee spiritual perspective. You, the spirit, are in charge, not the energies you use, so you must be careful of your intent and beliefs.

If you focus internally on yourself, as spirit, and God within, practicing and using spiritual techniques can be a wonderful experience. Whether you are using them to meditate or to create in daily life, you can have fun using them to create and communicate as spirit through your body. All it takes is desire, belief, perseverance, and a little determination. The greatest experience in life is to experience yourself, as spirit, and your God.

To practice the spiritual techniques presented in the following pages, find a quiet place where you can be alone for at least half an hour. Sit in a straight-backed chair with your hands separated in your lap and your feet separated and flat on the floor. This posture allows for the flow of both earth and cosmic energies and allows you to use your earth energy as you use kundalini energy. It also helps you ground. Sit as straight as possible, since your spine is the main channel for the flow of your energy. Keep a journal to record your experiences at the end of your meditations to validate your growth.

When you practice the following techniques, close your eyes and turn within to yourself, as spirit. Take some deep breaths and relax your body to let go of effort in your body. Allow the techniques to flow for you, as spirit. Enjoy the techniques, and let them help you to awaken to yourself, your creativity, and your God.

"The human body is a composite of the soul's information and concepts, so the soul is learning to take control of its own creativity."

Grounding: The Foundation

Grounding is the most important spiritual technique you can learn. It is the foundation on which all the other techniques are built. Grounding is the "rock" of spiritual techniques. Everything is energy and grounding is an energetic connector, similar to an electrical ground. It grounds the energy that is you to the energy that is planet Earth. Grounding is a simple spiritual technique. Do not let the simplicity of it keep you from seeing the power in grounding. You will discover that grounding creates a strong connection between you and your body, and you and the Earth. Grounding is essential for the controlled use of kundalini energy. You must ground to use your kundalini energy safely. Grounding is still my most important technique after over twenty years of spiritual work.

Your grounding connection keeps you in touch with your physical creations, including your body. This connection keeps you strong in the physical world. It connects you to the Earth the way your silver cord connects you to your body. If you are not grounded, you may feel spacey, out of touch, overly emotional, or afraid. Grounding gives you a strong presence in the physical world. This strengthening aspect of grounding is essential when running kundalini energy as kundalini can cause a sense of unreality or instability before you learn to control it.

Grounding helps you be in control of your first and second chakras which relate to physical reality, and emotionality and sexuality. It is extremely important to be in touch with and in some control of the lower chakras when you turn on and use your kundalini energy.[5] The kundalini stimulates what you have stored in the body, so you need to know what you have and how to deal with it. If you know you have pain related to your emotions, you will be ready to deal with it as it is released. If you are grounded, you will be in charge of the process.

Grounding gives you safety to create in the physical world. It helps you be in touch with what is real for the physical world such as time, space, mass, effort, and other physical characteristics. Grounding helps you differentiate between spirit and body realities so you can operate effectively in both realms of creativity. Grounding helps you focus on what you are doing so you are safer, just as you are safer when you drive a car if you are focused on what you are doing. Kundalini energy can draw your attention so strongly to the spiritual realm that your grounding becomes especially important since you use grounding to help you stay aware of what is happening in your physical world.

Grounding can also be used as a release of energy. You can let go of any unwanted or excess energy down your grounding cord. Everything is energy, and you can release energy down your grounding cord to remove it from your body and spiritual system. This release mechanism is helpful when you use kundalini energy as you stimulate a great deal of energy that you will want to release, and grounding provides an easy avenue to let go of the unwanted energy.

Grounding makes it possible to run kundalini energy in a safe, controlled manner. If you do not learn how to ground and practice grounding, you will have problems with kundalini energy. You may have some powerful and exciting experiences, but you will eventually create difficulties since you will not be in touch with your body and physical creations. As you awaken spiritually, you need to relearn how to walk before you relearn how to fly. Learn to ground, and you will enjoy your other spiritual techniques and abilities much more, including kundalini energy; you, the being, will be in charge of what is happening in your universe.

TO GROUND, sit in a chair with your spine as straight as possible, your hands and feet separate, and your feet flat on the floor. Close your eyes, take a few deep breaths and relax. Be aware of the area near the base of your spine. An energy center called the first chakra is located here that deals with how you relate to the physical world.

ALLOW A FLOW of energy to move from this energy center, near the base of your spine, to the center of the Earth. Be quiet with this flow of energy. Be sure that it is connected at your first chakra and flowing all the way to the center of the Earth and attached there.

SIT IN THIS POSTURE, with your grounding cord flowing from your first chakra to the center of the Earth. Allow time for your body to adjust to being grounded. Pay attention to your body's reaction to being grounded so you know what is happening in your physical world.

STAND AND WALK around the room grounded and notice how this feels. Sit down and be still with your grounding again and enjoy the experience of being connected and grounded to this reality.

BE STILL with your grounding cord for as long as you can. Practice grounding often to incorporate your grounding into your energetic system.

BE GROUNDED, at all times, and you will always have your spiritual foundation. Your breathing can help you relax and allow your grounding cord to flow.

Practice your grounding when you meditate, when you run earth and cosmic energies, and when you run kundalini energy. You can be grounded at all times. It is helpful to be grounded in daily life as well as when you meditate. You never stop being a creative spirit, and grounding helps you create consciously and safely. Practice grounding regularly, and it will soon become part of your way of operating in the world.

Grounding makes it safe for your body when you use all of the other spiritual techniques. Without grounding, your spiritual journey will be difficult and confusing, if not impossible. Practice grounding whenever you use the other techniques, and as often as you can, so you will be in control of the other techniques and of your energy.

KUNDALINI ENERGY
AND CLAIRVOYANCE

Your body is your temple and the center of your head is your throne room. The center of your head is the place where you, as spirit, see and know what is occurring in your world. It is where your clairvoyant ability is located and the place where you can be neutral about what you are creating. The center of your head is where you are able to see and control your universe. If you, the spirit, sit in any other place in the body, you do not have the same level of control or neutrality. If you are in your heart chakra, you are strongly influenced by the emotions of the body. If you are in any of the lower chakras, you are engulfed by the body's characteristics and circumstances.

The center of your head is where you can see, both physically and spiritually. The physical eyes are located in the head and the spiritual eye or clairvoyant chakra is located in the center of the head. This is the place to be if you want to see physically or spiritually. When you put your spiritual attention in the center of your head, it stimulates your clairvoyant abilities to help you see spiritual phenomena. This clear spiritual sight allows you to be neutral about what you have and what you are creating. Neutrality helps you have a spiritual perspective of life.

Kundalini energy stimulates clairvoyance. As it rises up the spine, it moves into and through the head and out the top of the head. The kundalini energy moves through the pineal gland at the top of the brain stem and stimulates this gland. The pineal is the gland associated with clairvoyance and the reflection of light in the body. The kundalini energy moving through the sixth chakra or clairvoyant energy center is what often causes people to see colors when they have a kundalini experience.

The experience of seeing colors comes from the clairvoyance being turned on by the flow of kundalini energy through the pineal gland and through the sixth or clairvoyant chakra, not from the kundalini energy itself. Kundalini energy does not always cause you to see colors, just as it does not always stimulate the clairvoyant abilities. It may stimulate disruptive energies stored in the sixth chakra to cleanse that chakra before clarity is experienced. Kundalini energy can be very helpful in cleansing and using your clairvoyance. If you focus within and use your clairvoyance to see yourself, instead of others, your kundalini energy is safer for you since you will be focused on yourself and what you know.

To tune into your clairvoyance, you need to be in the center of your head since the information about clairvoyant abilities is located there. Simply by putting your attention there, you will stimulate these abilities. You need to be in this neutral place when you run your kundalini energy since a great deal happens very rapidly. Your grounding and neutrality will help you to deal with the kundalini experience. Your clairvoyance helps you see what is occurring so you can learn from and be in control of the experience.

Kundalini energy stimulates all of your psychic abilities and all of your chakras. You need to be careful and move slowly in your healing process to avoid confusion or damage. Do not seek excitement or thrills with kundalini experiences. You will lose control of your spiritual awakening if you are not careful in dealing with your kundalini energy. Enjoy the process by taking personal responsibility for your kundalini experience instead of seeking excitement or power, and you can reap great rewards.

SIT IN a chair with your spine straight, your feet on the floor, and your hands in your lap. Take a few deep breaths to relax your body and help you sit up straight.

CLOSE your eyes, and turn within. Relax your body, and enjoy the quiet time for a moment.

ALLOW YOUR grounding to flow from your first chakra near the base of your spine to the center of the

Earth. Let your grounding be well connected at your first chakra and at the center of the Earth. Take a few moments to focus on your grounding cord and make it strong by increasing the flow of energy.

BE AWARE of yourself as spirit. You are a bright light. Focus your bright light into the center of your head. Be above and behind your physical eyes in the center of your head.

BE STILL in the center of your head. Experience being there for as long as you can.

SEE THE BRIGHT LIGHT that is you. If you do not see a bright light, allow time for you to focus into the center of your head. Ground and be still to allow you to come into the center of your head. This can happen quickly, or it may take months.

GROUNDING helps you be in the center of your head. Increase your grounding to help you be centered in your head. Let more energy flow down your grounding cord to make it easier for you to be in your head.

USE YOUR fingers to help you focus in your head. Touch one index finger to your temple and the other to your forehead, and imagine a line from each finger which intersect in the center of your head. Focus your attention

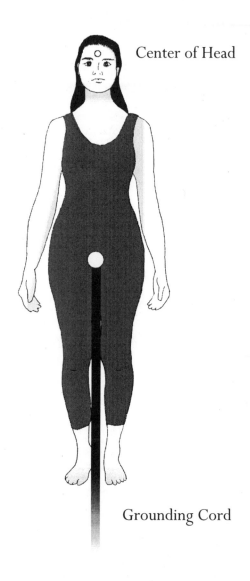

Center of Head

Grounding Cord

FIGURE 1: CENTER OF HEAD AND GROUNDING

to this spot, lower your hands, and be still in the center of your head.

BE IN the center of your head and be still.

Practice being in the center of your head when you meditate and whenever you think about it. The more you focus your attention into the center of your head, the more you will be focused on being neutral. This exercise also stimulates the use of your clairvoyant abilities. You need your clairvoyance when you turn on your kundalini; everything moves rapidly with kundalini and you need to see what is happening. Your ability to see clearly allows you to see what you have created from a neutral, non-judgmental perspective. This makes it possible for you to release the energy or experience easily, without judgment or hesitation. Without the use of your clairvoyance, you may spend unnecessary time and energy analyzing and holding on to the energy you are trying to release with your kundalini energy flow. Your clairvoyance can help you rise above your intellect and emotions so you, the spirit, can regain seniority with your body. The body may rebel against your spiritual power and attempt to stop it or at least block it, so use your grounding and centering in your head to be senior to your body.

Clairvoyance allows you to be neutral about and have a spiritual perspective of your kundalini experiences. Kundalini energy stimulates your clairvoyance and helps you cleanse and use this spiritual ability to see spiritual phenomena. Kundalini and clairvoyance are a powerful spiritual team. When you use them with a spiritual focus, you can use each ability to assist you with the other. You can use both abilities to help you operate as spirit in the physical world.

"The greatest experience in life is to experience yourself, as spirit, and your God."

SPIRITUAL PERSPECTIVE
AND CREATIVITY

You create rapid change when you use kundalini energy, so you need a spiritual perspective to correctly interpret what is happening to you and to stay on your path. You gain a spiritual perspective by grounding, focusing in the center of your head, using your clairvoyance, and keeping your attention focused on spirit instead of body. The ability to see spiritually is located in the sixth chakra, in the center of your head. This space contains your information on how to see spiritual phenomena such as auras, beings without bodies, and mental image pictures. Your clairvoyance helps you see truth and lies in yourself and others. It is important to see your own truth when your kundalini energy gets your system moving at warp speed. You need to make decisions rapidly, and your clairvoyance and spiritual perspective help you make neutral decisions.

You can easily misinterpret a kundalini experience or any other spiritual experience without your clairvoyance. You will consider the experience only in physical terms, if you do not use your spiritual sight, and may not create

KUNDALINI ENERGY: *The Flame of Life*

what you originally intended. For example, if you turn on your kundalini energy and see bright lights in your head and around you and do not recognize this as a spiritual phenomenon, you may go to see many advisors looking for answers. If you have already meditated and gotten in touch with your clairvoyance, you can see that your clairvoyance is being stimulated by your kundalini energy.

It is very important to meditate on your spiritual abilities before turning on your kundalini energy, so you will know what is happening to you when these spiritual abilities get stimulated. You will be in charge of your experience if you already know how to manipulate your clairvoyant talents to see what is occurring. When you see what is happening, you can take charge and create what you desire. If you cannot see, you may be afraid and move instead in the wrong direction.

Clairvoyance, healing energy, telepathy, telekinesis, precognition, clairaudience, and the many other psychic abilities can be developed by everyone. Psychic abilities do not guarantee a spiritual perspective and do not prove someone is a spiritual teacher or even spiritually focused. Kundalini energy does not guarantee a spiritual focus either. Kundalini does activate the chakra system which has information about all of the spiritual abilities, thus it is important to know the chakras and what they contain before you stimulate them. It is important to know what you want to create before you increase your vibration.

You, the spirit, create your spiritual focus with your desire and your belief. If you desire a spiritual perspective and believe you can have it, then you will. Combine this desire and belief with your spiritual abilities listed above and you move rapidly in your spiritual growth. Remember that you will get what you pray for and you may not like everything you see. You must learn to be personally responsible with all of your talents. If you use your techniques and talents to focus on power instead of spiritual perspective, you will have a different experience. What you desire and believe in, you will create. It is important to develop a spiritual perspective when using kundalini energy so you will follow your spiritual path.

I attended a psychic event several years ago and was amazed by the competitive nature of the psychic participants. Many of these people had spent time focusing on their clairvoyance and healing energy, but did not have a spiritual perspective. They used their abilities and techniques on a physical level, mostly focused on making money and being better than others. One clairvoyant reader loudly announced to me that she would be rich and famous, with the emphasis on rich. I experienced compassion toward this talented woman since she did not have a clue about the gifts she had or how to use them.

A spiritual perspective requires that you have some seniority with your body's characteristics such as competition, emotionality, sexuality, and pain. The spiritual techniques can be used to help you and your body to attain this seniority. Grounding, centering, and consciously using energies all help you gain spiritual seniority. You must learn to stay senior to the body's desires and emotions to maintain a spiritual view and create your spiritual desires.

Kundalini energy helps you be aware of and learn to know yourself and your abilities. Kundalini energy helps you focus on your spiritual nature. It does not guarantee a spiritual perspective, but definitely helps you create one if that is your desire. Kundalini also stimulates your sixth chakra which is the center of clairvoyance and the focus for spiritual perspective.

You can practice your clairvoyant abilities during meditation, or any time in your life. It is best to start by practicing in meditation so you gain control of the ability. Clairvoyance can soon become an important aspect of your life. Many people use their clairvoyance to create every aspect of their life. You can learn to use it to gain a spiritual perspective of you and the world around you. You can use your spiritual perspective to create as spirit in the physical world.

PRACTICE using your clairvoyance. Sit in a chair, feet flat on the floor, hands in your lap, and take a few deep breaths to relax your body.

GROUND from your first chakra, near the base of your spine, to the center of the Earth. Focus your attention as spirit, into the center of your head. Take a few moments to let your body adjust to you being grounded and centered in your head.

FROM THE CENTER OF YOUR HEAD, visualize the mental image picture of a rose, about six inches in front of your forehead. Admire your creation.

LET THE ROSE GO. You can let it melt away, explode it like a firecracker, or just let it disappear.

CREATE ANOTHER ROSE and let it go. Repeat creating and destroying a rose until you feel comfortable with the exercise.

CREATE A ROSE, put anything you no longer want into the rose, and explode both. Repeat creating and exploding what you do not want until it disappears. Creating and destroying roses allows you to release energy.

You are stimulating your clairvoyance and releasing energy by creating and letting go of roses. The rose is a neutral, spiritual symbol to use in the exercise. This exercise stimulates the apparatus in your head that relates to your clairvoyance. The exercise cleanses the clairvoyant apparatus and brings your clairvoyance into the present. The more you create and destroy roses, the clearer your clairvoyance becomes. You can turn on your kundalini energy without creating disturbance in your clairvoyant chakra, if you meditate on cleansing and owning your sixth chakra and clairvoyance first. You can also use your clairvoyance to see what is happening to you when you manipulate the powerful energies at your disposal.

Your clairvoyance is important to develop in relation to your meditation, especially your kundalini meditation, since clairvoyance lets you see what is, so that you can relate to the present reality. If you operate from lies, other people's information, past-time information, or anything other than the present truth for you, your spiritual awakening will be disturbed by these influences. Clairvoyance is essential for following your spiritual path so you can see where you have been and where you are going.[6]

When you create and let go of roses, you are releasing energy from your system. When you run kundalini energy, you release energy from your system. Both techniques help you cleanse and heal your spiritual and physical systems. The technique of creating and destroying roses is more gentle than running kundalini energy. Running kundalini is more powerful, faster, and does not involve the intellect. When you use your clairvoyance to see what you are changing, you can get involved in judging or intellectualizing what you see. When you run kundalini energy, there is no time for thought since the energy moves too fast for the intellect to relate to it.

If you find that your body needs a break from kundalini energy, you can use the technique of creating and destroying roses to continue your healing in a gentler manner. This technique of releasing energy and cleansing will create a powerful healing also. It is slower and takes longer than kundalini energy and is more in affinity with the body since the body takes time to change and kundalini is fast. Using your clairvoyance to create and destroy roses is a healing way to spiritualize your system. You develop a spiritual perspective about your creativity.

Your spiritual perspective is enhanced every time you focus on your clairvoyance and create and let go of roses. Your neutrality and your ability to see your own truth grows with every meditation using this technique. Your spiritual perspective is essential when you begin to use your kundalini energy since your physical perspective cannot give you the information you need. Meditation, kundalini energy, and clairvoyance are all spiritual phenomena about which your body may not have information. You, the spirit, must use your spiritual abilities to gain your spiritual perspective. With it, you can see your way to create what you are here to do.

Practice grounding, centering in your head, and creating and letting go of roses often. These techniques cleanse your body and prepare it for higher vibrations. Meditation heals the body so you can use it most effectively as well as bring more of your energy into and through your body. Use the techniques to prepare your body to use kundalini energy in a safe and gentle manner. Develop your clairvoyance so you can see what you are creating and where you are going.

"We never reach a perfect state of being, simply an awakened state so we can respond spiritually to what is. Only God is perfect."

MANIPULATING ENERGIES
TO MEDITATE

Everything is energy. There are many forms or vibrations of energy. Some energy is a high vibration which cannot be seen by the physical eyes and some is a low, slow vibration that we can physically see. Energies can be manipulated to use for our meditations, creativity, health, communication, and every experience in life. Some energies are easier to work with than others. The more intense the vibration, the greater the challenge is to control the energy. Kundalini energy is a very high vibration, so it is advisable to learn to manipulate other energies before playing with kundalini. One is responsible for whatever one creates, regardless of what energy is used.

Earth energy is the energy we have invested in planet Earth. It is a slower vibration available for us to use in our creativity on Earth. We can draw from this pool of energy at any time and place. The physical body is made up of energy invested in the Earth, so the body has a great deal of affinity for earth energy. Earth energy is an easy vibration to learn to manipulate as the body feels comfortable with it. Earth energy also helps the body feel safe as you deal with higher vibrations.

Cosmic energy is the creative power we draw from the Cosmos to form our material world. We use cosmic energy to create and to cleanse our creations. Cosmic energy is unlimited. It is spiritual energy not bound in matter. Cosmic energy is infinite, and we can learn to manipulate it for our spiritual creativity in a body. Cosmic energy is a higher vibration than earth energy and takes more practice and focus to learn how to manipulate. Cosmic energy consists of an infinite variety of vibrations that can be translated into color. We can use any color for our meditations. Practice helps one to understand the effect of different color vibrations on your system. Play with colors and learn to know them. There are no rules about which colors to use.

Using earth and cosmic energies during meditation helps you experience and adjust to differences between spirit and body. These energies help you balance the dichotomy of spirit and body as you create in a body. You learn to use both the spiritual and physical characteristics available to you by consciously using the earth and cosmic energies. As you learn to manipulate these energies, you gain control over your creativity in the physical realm. Both energies help you gain spiritual seniority with your body.

Earth energy helps you relate to the Earth and to your body. It helps you to be grounded in the physical world so you do not get out of touch with your body and other physical creations. Earth energy enhances your grounding technique and makes your body feel real so you do not need to use inappropriate energies, such as pain, to do this. Earth energy gives your body stability as you increase your vibration and focus on your spiritual abilities. Earth energy and grounding give you the foundation you need to manifest your high spiritual energy into your body safely.

Cosmic energy provides you with vitality, spiritual perspective, and infinite creative power. Cosmic energy is the life force with which you, as spirit, create. You can increase your creativity and energy a great deal by consciously manipulating cosmic energy through your system. You can revitalize your body and enhance the vitality of all of your creations. Cosmic energy is a powerful force that you can learn to manipulate for healing, creating, and communicating through your body. Cosmic energy enhances your spiritual perspective and helps you operate more fully as spirit in your body.

You can prepare to use your kundalini energy by learning to use earth and cosmic energies. When you use kundalini energy, the earth energy is very helpful in stabilizing the body and enhancing the grounding. You can eventually learn to use all three energies at the same time. The new student needs to spend time practicing with grounding, centering, and running earth and cosmic energies before moving on to use kundalini energy. You gain seniority as spirit with your body by learning to manipulate these energies first. When you do turn on your kundalini energy, you have a foundation of communication and cleansing with your body. You also have another technique for continued healing if the kundalini energy becomes too intense and must be turned down or off for a time.

PRACTICE RUNNING YOUR ENERGY by sitting in a chair with your back straight, your feet on the floor, and your hands separated in your lap. Take a few deep breaths to relax your body.

GROUND from your first chakra, near the base of your spine, to the center of the Earth. Breathe deeply, and let your breath help you send energy down your grounding cord. Take a few minutes to focus on your grounding.

BE IN THE CENTER OF YOUR HEAD. Focus your attention as spirit into the center of your head, above and behind your eyes. Be still in the center of your head for a few moments to allow your body to adjust to your high spiritual energy.

SEE YOURSELF as a bright light of energy in the center of your head.

SAY HELLO to your body and let it experience you

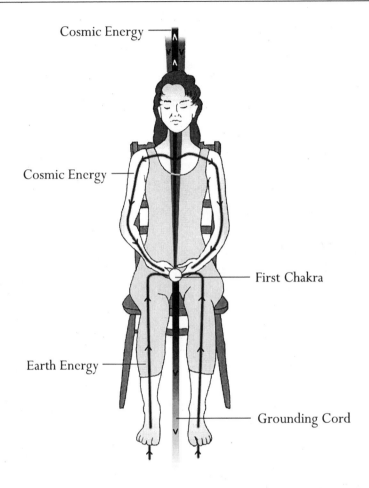

Cosmic Energy

Cosmic Energy

First Chakra

Earth Energy

Grounding Cord

FIGURE 2: RUNNING EARTH AND COSMIC ENERGIES

Earth energy runs up through the leg channels from the Earth. Cosmic energy runs down the back channels, mixes with Earth energy at the first chakra, runs up the front channels and down the arm channels. Energy grounds off down the grounding cord.

grounding and focusing in your head.

FROM THIS grounded, centered state, tune into your feet. There are energy centers in the arches of your feet. Allow the energy centers to open like the lens of a camera. Let earth energy flow up through the energy centers in your feet, through channels in your legs, to your first chakra near the base of your spine, and then flow down your grounding cord.

BE STILL and let the earth energy flow through your system. Experience the stabilizing effect of this energy on your body and the enhancement of your grounding.

You can use earth energy all of the time. This energy is in affinity with your body and helps you use your body effectively. Practice using earth energy in your meditations and during your daily life to help you get into the habit of using it. Once you have mastered using earth energy, you will feel more comfortable manipulating the higher vibrations.

PRACTICE USING COSMIC ENERGY. First focus on being grounded and centered in your head. Make sure your earth energy is moving from the energy centers in your feet, up the channels in your legs, to your first chakra near the base of your spine, and down your grounding cord.

EXPERIENCE THE GROUNDING and earth energy stabilizing your body. Focus in the center of your head so you will remain in charge of your energy flow.

BE AWARE of the top of your head. Gather cosmic energy into a ball above your head, and let the energy from the concentrated ball flow down through the top of your head, toward the back of your head, and through energy channels that run along each side of your spine.

AT THE FIRST CHAKRA, let the cosmic energy mix with your earth energy and move up channels that go through the body to the top of your head. Let the energy flow out the top of your head and fountain all around your body.

ALLOW SOME OF THE ENERGY to flow from the cleft of your throat through channels in your shoulders and arms and out the palms of your hands.

BE STILL and enjoy the flow of cosmic energy through your system. Feel the energy flow into the top of your head. Feel it flow down your back channels, and up your front channels, and out the top of your head. Feel it flow around your body and out your arms and hands.

BE QUIET with the flow of earth and cosmic energies

moving through your body and energy system. Let the energies do the cleansing and energizing without effort.

STILL YOUR MIND and let the energy flow. Increase your grounding to help you be still. Continue running your energies as long as possible. Thirty minutes is beneficial as it gives the body time to relax, be quiet, and heal.

You can take charge of your spiritual and physical systems by consciously running earth and cosmic energies. These energies are available for you to manipulate to create what you need. You can use them to balance your spirit and body dichotomy, to increase your spirit and body communication, and to gain control of your creativity through the body. It is important to practice using earth and cosmic energies in your meditations before you begin to use your kundalini energy. These energies help you, as spirit, gain seniority with your body and learn how to consciously manipulate energies through your physical system. You will have more control with the intense kundalini energy if you first learn to manipulate the less intense earth and cosmic energies.

You learned to walk before you learned to run. You learned to drive a car slowly before you drove it fast. You need to approach your spiritual work in the same way. You need to start slowly, to give you the opportunity to learn about your body, your creations, and your unique spiritual vibration. You need to get to know your strengths and weaknesses so you can be in charge of your creative process. You will have a great deal more fun and success if you open to your spiritual powers and abilities slowly and gently.

You will create a healing relationship with your body if you allow it the time it needs to adjust to the changes you are creating within it. Whenever you run your earth and cosmic energies, you create changes in your body and it needs time to adjust to those changes. You create harmony with your body by allowing it time for its growth. It must adjust to you taking conscious charge of it.

Meditation can be fun and rewarding. Take time for meditating every day and you will reap the rewards. You will learn to know yourself as spirit and your creative process through your body. You will discover your purpose here on Earth and learn to fulfill it. Use the spiritual techniques daily and you will be operating as spirit every day.

Have fun.

RUNNING KUNDALINI ENERGY

Kundalini energy is very powerful and needs to be used with respect. You need to be aware you are turning on a great force within yourself when you consciously turn on kundalini energy. Grounding and being centered in your head are essential techniques to use to create a safe and controlled experience with kundalini energy. You need to train yourself to be grounded and centered, and to run earth and cosmic energies before you begin running your kundalini energy. These techniques provide a firm foundation on which to build your spiritual house.

Kundalini energy is the transformer. It is helpful for you to know yourself before you begin using kundalini energy so you will know what you are transforming. If you have created illness or injury in your body, you will be healing these past experiences. You will have better control of your experience if you know that you are healing these painful experiences. Your communication with your body, to reassure it during the transformation, helps the process. You can let your body know that you are clearing past experiences and not creating new ones.

The body will resist the process if it does not know that the energy is coming out instead of coming in. Past life experiences can be especially disturbing if you are not grounded and centered, since your body will not have experienced them. You have to maintain your spiritual perspective during your kundalini experiences to be safe. You must take responsibility for your creations so you do not get off track blaming others or judging yourself.

Kundalini energy creates healing and raises vibrations. You can do a great deal with this energy in a short time so it is important to use it gently. You do not need to run a lot of kundalini to accomplish a great deal of healing. The body takes time to adjust to energetic changes. It helps to begin slowly and gently so the body does not get disturbed and try to stop your work. Allow a minimum of thirty minutes for your meditation since you need to let your kundalini energy run at least twenty minutes before turning it off. This meditation requires time and attention. When you run a great deal of kundalini energy, your body may gently sway back and forth. This is a natural result of the pulse of kundalini moving through your body.

The spine contains the main channel through the body for kundalini energy. The spine carries the nerves for communication from the brain to all parts of the body; it holds the body upright, it supports the head, and it is a very important part of the physical system. Consciously cleansing and healing the spine is a helpful place to start on your kundalini journey since it carries kundalini up through your body and spiritual system.

GROUND from your first chakra to the center of the Earth. Focus your attention into the center of your head. Be still and adjust to being grounded and centered in your head.

FROM THE CENTER OF YOUR HEAD, be aware of your feet chakras and open them. Let the earth energy flow up through your feet chakras, through the channels in your legs, to your first chakra, and down your grounding cord.

CREATE a ball of cosmic energy above your head and let the cosmic energy flow down to the top of your head, down channels on each side of your spine, to the first chakra.

MIX the earth and cosmic energies at the first chakra, and allow them to flow up through the channels running through your body, and fountain out the top of your head, and flow around your body.

LET some of the energy branch off at the cleft of your throat, flow through channels in your shoulders and arms, and out the palms of your hands.

BE STILL as you ground, center in your head, and let your earth and cosmic energies run.

CREATE AND LET GO OF a rose. Repeat creating and destroying roses for a few minutes to cleanse your head and help your energy flow.

Your preparation to run kundalini energy can take as little as ten minutes or as much as an hour or more, depending on your state of being. Do not judge the time it takes you to prepare your system. See yourself as you are and respond to what you and your body need, instead of operating from what you expect of yourself. The more you use spiritual techniques, the easier it is for you to operate as spirit in the physical world. The techniques also help you reach a state of meditation where you can communicate more easily as spirit.

You will know when you are ready to turn on your kundalini energy. The more you practice with all of your techniques, the more certain you will become about how to use them. Your body will become adjusted to the higher energy and work with you better every day. Manipulating energy has some similarities to starting an exercise program. The body may resist, at first, but eventually enjoys the healing process. Practicing every day is important to help you get in the habit and to train the body.

INCREASE YOUR GROUNDING. Grounding is very important when you use kundalini energy. Take a few minutes and focus on the energy flowing from your first chakra to the center of the Earth.

BE IN THE CENTER OF YOUR HEAD. Your clairvoyance is important when you use kundalini energy to help you maintain your neutral spiritual perspective. From the center of your head, you can be neutral about the energy that kundalini stimulates.

CONTINUE to run your earth energy. Let it flow up through your feet chakras, leg channels, to your first chakra, and down your grounding cord. This will enhance your grounding and help you be in touch with the physical world.

TAKE YOUR ATTENTION off of your cosmic energy for now. Let the excess flow down your grounding cord. It will gently flow, but you want to use much less cosmic energy while you learn to run kundalini energy. Diminishing the cosmic energy allows you to be more aware of the kundalini energy until you learn to identify it. This also keeps you from running too much energy through your body.

CREATE AND LET GO of several roses to clear your head. Your body will become accustomed to higher energy through time, and you can eventually run both the cosmic and kundalini energies. Start by focusing on the kundalini energy.

FROM THE CENTER OF YOUR HEAD, put your attention on the base of your spine. Be aware of the coccyx at the tip of the spine.

CREATE A ROSE and explode it to clear anything at the base of your spine. Create and release several roses to cleanse your entire spine.

CREATE A ROSE and move it to the tip of your spine and slowly move it up through your spine to the top. Put the rose six to eight inches in front of your forehead and explode it. This will clear the spine and release the energy stored there. Let the rose completely fill the spine to cleanse it inside and out. Repeat this cleansing process several times.

FOCUS IN THE CENTER OF YOUR HEAD. Increase your grounding.

SAY HELLO TO YOUR KUNDALINI ENERGY at the base of your spine. Let the kundalini energy uncoil and slowly move up through the channel in the center of your spine. Move the energy slowly and gently.

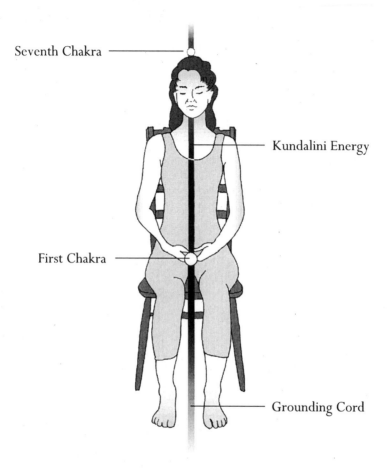

Seventh Chakra

Kundalini Energy

First Chakra

Grounding Cord

FIGURE 3: RUNNING KUNDALINI ENERGY

Kundalini energy flows up from the base of your spine, near the first chakra, through the channel in your spine, and out the top of your head above the spine. Energy grounds off down the grounding cord.

BE STILL, in the center of your head, and let the kundalini energy flow up the channel in your spine, and out the top of your head above the spine. Allow several minutes for the energy to begin flowing. Allow the time you need for it to flow all the way up and out the top of your head. The time you need varies a great deal from person to person.

FEEL THE WARMTH of the energy as it flows up your spine and out the top of your head. Let the kundalini energy gently melt away any interference to its flow. Let the kundalini melt blocks and repair breaks in the channel in the spine so it flows smoothly.

BE STILL AND ENJOY the flow of kundalini energy.

MAKE SURE the energy is flowing all the way up your spine and out the top of your head. Take the time for the energy to move all the way up the spine. If the energy stops or slows at any spot along the spine, let the kundalini energy gently melt away the interference.

CREATE AND LET GO OF ROSES to help you move out any interference to the kundalini flow. Creating and exploding roses helps you as you begin running your kundalini energy since so much is occurring. As you adjust, you can use kundalini energy without blowing roses.

BE GROUNDED and in the center of your head and experience the kundalini energy moving up your spine and out the top of your head. Be quiet and let it happen.

RUN YOUR KUNDALINI energy at least twenty minutes at a time. Once you have turned it on, let it flow for a minimum of twenty minutes or your body may become angry with you for turning it on and off.

If you have difficulty being still for twenty minutes, focus on your grounding and your kundalini flow, and let your thoughts float by instead of focusing on them. Do not resist your body; let it be as it is and focus on your spiritual system. Kundalini energy helps the body be still so you can meditate for a longer period of time and focus on yourself as spirit. The body rapidly learns to like kundalini energy since it is cleansing and relaxing if no disruption is stimulated. It helps you move above body pulls, such as the intellect and emotions, so you can operate on a more spiritual level. This helps the body be quiet and accept you as spirit. Kundalini energy provides a space for you, the spirit, to work in your physical body.

Kundalini energy moves so rapidly you transcend the intellect and function on a spiritual level. You do not need to create and destroy roses since the kundalini moves the energy. You can use the rose technique if you get stuck on something that blocks your kundalini flow;

otherwise, the kundalini energy will cleanse your system. You can create and destroy roses to speed up the cleansing process by using both techniques at once. You need to adjust to using your kundalini alone before you increase your healing level by combining techniques.

You do not eliminate your body issues by running kundalini energy. You spiritualize your physical system so you can deal with the body from a higher vibration. For example, you do not eliminate anger; you use your kundalini energy to move your anger through your system as a healing flow instead of throwing it at someone else or yourself. The body still has all of its emotions; you learn to deal with them from a more spiritual level. The body still has its intellect; you use kundalini energy to use or move above the intellect for your spiritual purpose.

Kundalini energy is to spiritualize the physical system for it to be more fully used by you, as spirit. It does not eliminate the physical system. You still have emotions, sexuality, intellect, pain, and so forth; you use kundalini to raise the body to a higher vibration to be used by you, the spirit. Kundalini energy transforms your physical system into a higher vibration for your spiritual use. Eventually, the emotions, sexuality, intellect, survival instincts, and other body characteristics diminish in significance.

With kundalini energy, you use spiritual energy instead of physical energy and release physical limits. You operate without effort instead of with effort. You move above the hold of time and experience a spiritual timelessness. Your sense of space expands to eliminate limits. You experience your immortality, spiritual sight, and power. You tune into your ability to know and communicate with all things. Kundalini energy can help you reach a spiritual state of peace and harmony.

TUNE INTO YOUR KUNDALINI ENERGY. Notice if it is still flowing through your spine. Do you feel a warmth moving up your spine? Do you feel it moving out the top of your head?

INCREASE YOUR GROUNDING. You are using more energy in your body now and need increased grounding to balance the higher vibration.

BE STILL WITH YOUR KUNDALINI energy and notice how it is affecting your body. How does your body feel? Does it feel good? Does any part of it feel uncomfortable? Use your kundalini energy to move out any discomfort. Your body can be your guide to how things are working.

TALK WITH YOUR BODY about what you are doing and listen to what is happening with it. What is its main emotion while you run kundalini? Learn to know your body and what you have created in it.

SPEND TIME talking with your body to help it adjust to kundalini energy and to help you know what needs your attention. Allow your kundalini energy to move out any disturbance your body expresses.

WORK WITH YOUR BODY and your body will work with you. This is important as you begin so you learn about yourself and stay in control as spirit.

CONTROL your kundalini flow. Create a dial from 0-10, and see how much kundalini energy you are running. Beginners, turn your dial to five or below, to allow your body adjustment time.

PLAY with the dial; beginners move between 1-5, and those who have used kundalini for over a year, turn your energy up and down slowly from 1-9.

BE AWARE of how different levels of kundalini energy affect you and your body. You can use more when meditating than when doing other things. Turn to the most comfortable setting for you and your body. Always consider the body since it is your vessel.

PUT YOUR DIAL IN A ROSE and explode it when you are through experimenting with your kundalini flow. Create a new dial each time you adjust your kundalini energy.

Your body makes a great deal of change rapidly when you run kundalini energy. When you begin, you need to regularly talk with your body during your kundalini meditations so you know what is happening in your body. If you stimulate pain, you need to know this so you can complete your cycle of healing and not carry the stimulated pain with you after your meditation. Know what is happening in your body and you know what is happening in your world. Knowledge brings you greater power and eventually more control. You can graduate to a place of silence and peace after you learn how your system works.

You can use your kundalini energy to heal anything. You can use it to move out pain, past experiences, or any emotion such as fear, hate, or jealousy. You can use kundalini energy to enhance energy such as affinity, compassion, or love. Kundalini energy is a high vibration and can be used to increase or to remove energy. You are the one who decides what energies you wish to clear and what energies you want to enhance. You are spirit and the one in charge of all of your energies, including kundalini energy.

It is extremely important to know how to turn off your kundalini energy. When you know how to turn your kundalini energy on and off, you are in control of it. You, as spirit, are meant to be in control of all of your energies as they are tools for you to use in your creative process. Knowing how to turn your kundalini energy off is as important as turning it on.

TO TURN OFF YOUR KUNDALINI ENERGY, start by being grounded and in the center of your head.

VISUALIZE A SMALL ICE BLUE BALL OF ENERGY above the kundalini flow coming out of the top of your head. Slowly move the ice blue ball of energy down to the top of your head, through your head to your spine, and down your spine.

SLOWLY move the ice blue energy all the way down your spine to the base of your spine. Let the cool blue energy put out the fire of the kundalini energy. Let the kundalini energy rest. Let it coil up and go to sleep.

CREATE A GOLD BALL OF ENERGY above your head and let it follow the blue ball of energy down your spine. Let the gold energy neutralize and cleanse your spine. Move the gold energy all the way to the tip of your spine and down your grounding cord.

SAY GOOD NIGHT to your kundalini energy and put it to sleep.

FOCUS ON YOUR GROUNDING and be in the center of your head. Take a few deep breaths to adjust your system and relax your body. Make sure your earth energy is running up your leg channels to your first chakra and down your grounding cord.

TUNE INTO YOUR COSMIC ENERGY and let it flow down the channels along the outside of your spine to your first chakra, and back up the channels in your body to the top of your head, and fountain all around you.

LET THE ENERGY FLOW down channels in your arms and out the palms of your hands.

RELAX AND LET your earth and cosmic energies flow for a few moments to allow your system to adjust to this level of energy.

CREATE AND LET GO of roses to release energy and help you return to your usual level of energy. Release excess energy down your grounding cord as well.

BEND FORWARD and release energy from your head, arms, and shoulders. Sit up straight and take a few deep breaths to end your meditation.

You may want to stretch and bend after your meditation to release energy from your body. Pay attention to how you feel after your meditations and you will learn a great deal about yourself. Kundalini energy is a powerful force so you need to be aware of how it is affecting your body. You need to determine whether you need to turn it up, down, on or off. You have to be in touch with your body and environment to know what you need to do for optimum beneficial use.

One of the many beautiful aspects of kundalini energy is that it is unique to you. No one else's kundalini energy is like yours and no one else runs their energy the way you do. You do not want to compete with anyone else about kundalini energy as everyone is unique in his or her use of this spiritual energy. You will disrupt your flow of kundalini energy if you attempt to run it like someone else. If you read or hear about other people's kundalini experiences, be sure to allow them their experiences and let yourself have your own. Spirit is unique and kundalini energy is a high spiritual vibration.

You can create a wonderful experience by using your kundalini energy in a gentle, responsible manner. Kundalini can help you return to your spiritual awareness, awaken your abilities, release limits, and be all that you are meant to be. Kundalini energy can help you raise your vibration in your body for clear communication with God.

CREATING IN AN AWAKENED STATE OF CONSCIOUSNESS

Spirit can create an awakened state of consciousness in the physical body. Some beings have accomplished this, some are in the process, and others are still asleep to the fact that they are spirit. Kundalini energy helps you awaken to your spirituality. Being awake can be a great joy. Some experience difficulties waking up and others do not. Every soul has its unique experience. If you do have challenges to move through, you can use them to strengthen yourself.

An awakened state of being does not mean that you do not have a physical life. Being awake allows you to see that you are spirit, not your body, and that everything you do or experience is your creation, including your physical creations. By waking up to the fact that you are spirit and the creator of your reality, you regain your personal power. When you accept that you are spirit and in charge of your life, you are again in control of your creativity. This awakened state requires that you take complete responsibility for yourself and all of your creations. You are not responsible for anyone else, only for yourself and what you create. This means you are responsible for your actions, thoughts, and creations. You are not responsible for what anyone else does, thinks, or creates. You are totally responsible for yourself.

One way to determine your level of personal responsibility is to ask yourself some questions and answer the questions by visualizing a gauge from 0-100 and allowing the gauge to register the percentage after each question.

- How much do you blame others for events in your life?
- What percentage do you believe you are a victim to someone or something?
- How much do you try to control others?
- How much do you believe that you are in charge of your life?
- How much do you take responsibility for your actions?

A high percentage on questions one through three and a low percentage on questions four and five indicates a low degree of personal responsibility. The percentages will change as you grow and mature spiritually. You will need to be personally responsible to continue your spiritual awakening. Any time you catch yourself blaming others, being a victim, controlling others, or not being responsible for yourself, you can use your grounding, centering, and kundalini energy flow to help you clear these lies and take charge of your creativity. Letting yourself make mistakes is an aspect of being personally responsible. No one is perfect, and you need to make mistakes to learn.

The awakened state of consciousness allows each individual soul creative space. Everyone is meant to be free, and kundalini can help you attain your spiritual freedom. Personal responsibility for you and your creations helps you create your independence from all things so you can develop being whole within yourself. If you blame, play victim games, or do not take responsibility for yourself in any way, you give away your power. You do not have a spiritual perspective if you are not owning what you create. You divide yourself and cannot follow the kundalini path of spiritual wholeness. Kundalini awakens your spiritual nature, your abilities, what you have created, and clears limits to your creativity. Caution must be used in this process to avoid the temptations of the ego. You may feel like an invincible god when you run kundalini energy, and you need to remember that your creative realm is within your personal space and does not include anyone or anything but you.

When you are spiritually awake, you see yourself and everyone else as spirit. You learn to respect every other soul's personal space and own your personal creative space. You become so involved in your creative process that you do not invade or harm others. You see all souls as creative, independent, and with the ability to be whole. You see everyone as a part of God.

This spiritual view is greatly enhanced by using kundalini energy. Everyday life brings challenges to disrupt this view and introduce the physical perspective. It takes time, commitment, desire, and belief to maintain an awakened state. Kundalini energy makes the process easier and more fun if used correctly.

A talented friend of mine was recently challenged to have a spiritual perspective. She was scheduled to lead a spiritual group, and it became clear that she was not ready to take that step. I helped her see that it could be disturbing to her and the group. She was angry. Quickly she used her kundalini energy to clear ego from her space and regained her amusement. This woman teaches classes on kundalini energy and is spiritually aware, and still had the temptation to do what her ego wanted instead of following a beneficial path. We have to stay constantly vigilant to stay on our spiritual path once we begin using kundalini energy. We never reach a perfect state of being, simply an awakened state so we can respond spiritually to what is. Only God is perfect.

Kundalini energy is a powerful, spiritual energy available to us to help us awaken as spirit in the physical body. It can help us undivide and become whole. It can assist in our healing, growth, and increased awareness. Kundalini energy can be used to awaken to our god-self and our part in the Cosmic Whole.

Enjoy waking up and continue to rejoice through the challenges and ecstasies of being awake.

FOOTNOTE REFERENCES

[1]   *Earth Energy: The Spiritual Frontier* by Mary Ellen Flora, 1996.

[2]   *Chakras: Key to Spiritual Opening* by Mary Ellen Flora, 1993.

[3] See note 1

[4] *Male & Female Energies: The Balancing Act* by Mary Ellen Flora, 1997.

[5] See note 2

[6] *Clairvoyance: Key to Spiritual Perspective* by Mary Ellen Flora, 1992.

INDEX

Mary Ellen Flora has devoted her life to inspiring others, from teaching pre-kindergarten to high school, to teaching spirituality. For the last 23 years she has taught with amusement, love, and neutrality as she inspires and assists others to wake up to their spiritual nature.

This same devotion can be found in her writing. She is the author of the Key Series of books and audio tapes and the Energy Series of books. The information contained in each book is presented clearly and with amusement. Each book assists you in discovering your spiritual path and your self-healing. The four-volume Key series focuses on Meditation, Healing, Clairvoyance and Chakras. The Energy Series consists of four titles: *Cosmic Energy, Earth Energy, Male and Female Energies*, and *Kundalini Energy*.

Mary Ellen resides in the Pacific Northwest with her husband, M.F. "Doc" Slusher. Their dedication to spiritual freedom led to the co-founding of the Church of Divine Man and the CDM Psychic Institute, a non-profit organization. Currently there are seven locations on the West Coast of the United States and Canada dedicated to teaching and encouraging individuals to focus on spiritual growth, self healing, and clairvoyance.

CDM Publications is a small press offering books and tapes of a spiritual nature. Our publications offer information to assist you in awakening to yourself as spirit. Each publication offers easy-to-understand information on an aspect of spirituality and includes techniques to assist you in experiencing yourself as spirit.

CDM Publications
2402 Summit Avenue
Everett, WA 98201

Phone: (425) 259-9322
Toll Free: 1-800-360-6509
Fax: (425) 259-5109
E-mail: cdm@c-d-m.org
Website: www.c-d-m.org

If you have questions or are interested in learning more about meditation, clairvoyance or other topics concerning spiritual awareness, please contact us.

OTHER BOOKS OFFERED BY CDM PUBLICATIONS

by Mary Ellen Flora

The **Key Series:** books and tapes

Meditation: Key to Spiritual Awakening
Healing: Key to Spiritual Balance
Clairvoyance: Key to Spiritual Perspective
Chakras: Key to Spiritual Opening

The **Energy Series:** books

Cosmic Energy: The Creative Power
Earth Energy: The Spiritual Frontier
Male and Female Energies: The Balancing Act
Kundalini Energy: The Flame of Life

by M. F. "Doc" Slusher

I Believe: *Sermons*

All titles available from **CDM Publications**

CDM Publications
2402 Summit Avenue, Everett, WA 98201
Phone (425) 259-9322   Fax (425) 259-5109   Toll Free 1-800-360-6509

THE ENERGY SERIES BOOKS
by Mary Ellen Flora

Quantity Total

Cosmic Energy: *The Creative Power* — $12.00 US / $16.00 Canadian — ___ ___
Earth Energy: *The Spiritual Frontier* — $12.00 US / $16.00 Canadian — ___ ___
Male & Female Energies: *The Balancing Act* — $15.00 US / $21.00 Canadian — ___ ___
Kundalini Energy: *The Flame of Life* — $20.00 US / $25.00 Canadian — ___ ___
Kundalini Energy: *The Flame of Life* (Hardbound Edition) — $40.00 US / $50.00 Canadian — ___ ___

THE KEY SERIES BOOKS
by Mary Ellen Flora

Meditation: *Key to Spiritual Awakening* — $7.95 US / $11.00 Canadian — ___ ___
Healing: *Key to Spiritual Balance* — $7.95 US / $11.00 Canadian — ___ ___
Clairvoyance: *Key to Spiritual Perspective* — $10.00 US / $14.00 Canadian — ___ ___
Chakras: *Key to Spiritual Opening* — $10.00 US / $14.00 Canadian — ___ ___

THE KEY SERIES AUDIO CASSETTES
by Mary Ellen Flora

Meditation: *Key to Spiritual Awakening* — $9.95 US / $14.00 Canadian — ___ ___
Healing: *Key to Spiritual Balance* — $9.95 US / $14.00 Canadian — ___ ___
Clairvoyance: *Key to Spiritual Perspective* — $10.00 US / $14.00 Canadian — ___ ___
Chakras: *Key to Spiritual Opening* — $10.00 US / $14.00 Canadian — ___ ___

OTHER BOOKS AVAILABLE

I Believe: *Sermons* by M. F. "Doc" Slusher — $15.00 US / $21.00 Canadian — ___ ___
I Believe: *Sermons (Hardbound Edition)* — $30.00 US / $42.00 Canadian — ___ ___
CDM Hymnal — $15.00 US / $21.00 Canadian — ___ ___

SHIPPING & HANDLING:
$3.00 first item, 75c each additional item
Prices and availability subject to change without notice. Please allow 6 weeks for delivery.
No cash or COD.

Sub-Total ___
Shipping & Handling ___
Tax (8.3% WA residents only) ___
TOTAL ___

☐ VISA   ☐ MasterCard   ☐ Call me for credit information - Phone _____

Card # _____   Exp. Date _____

Signature _____

Name _____

Address _____

City _____   State _____   Zip _____